The universe is big. It's vast and complicated and ridiculous. And sometimes, very rarely, impossible things just happen and we call them miracles.

— The Doctor
Season 5, Episode 12

As it was in the beginning, is now, and ever shall be, world without end. *Bigger on the Inside: Christianity and Doctor Who* tells the story about a "Doctor" who transcends time and space so that humanity (his favorite beings) might live new and transformed lives. This exploration of *Doctor Who* lore not only unearths similar beliefs to historical Christianity, but also demonstrates that God can speak through anyone, anywhere, for any reason, at any time—no matter if it is 6 B.C., 2015 A.D., or even 5.5/Apple/26.

—Eric Bumpus
Founder of ReelTheology.com

DOCTOR: You betrayed me. You betrayed my trust, you betrayed our friendship, you betrayed everything I ever stood for. You let me down.
CLARA: Then why are you helping me?
DOCTOR: Why? Do you think I care for you so little that betraying me would make a difference?

—*Dark Water*
Season 8, Episode 11

Jesus often invites people, normal everyday people, to join him on a journey of transformation, service, love, and, at times, suffering. Jesus has a way of entering our lives and completely changing our worldview. *Bigger on the Inside: Christianity and Doctor Who* invites us all to enter the TARDIS and, like many of the Doctor's Companions over the years, have our worldview expanded to include all of Time and Space. Whether you are a fisherman like James and John or a department store clerk like Rose—are you ready to accept the invitation?"

—Ivan Strong Moore
CCO Campus Minister/strongmoores.wordpress.com

COPPER: Doctor, it must be well past midnight, Earth time. Christmas Day.
DOCTOR: So it is. Merry Christmas.
ASTRID: This Christmas thing, what's it all about?
DOCTOR: Long story. I should know, I was there. I got the last room.

—*Voyage of the Damned*
Season 4, Christmas Special

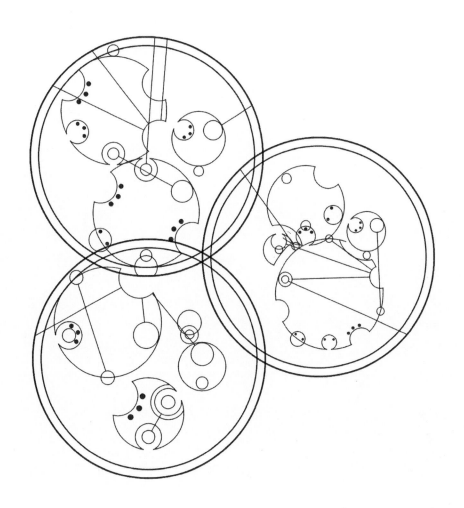

BIGGER ON THE INSIDE: CHRISTIANITY AND *DOCTOR WHO*

BIGGER ON THE INSIDE: CHRISTIANITY AND *DOCTOR WHO*

EDITED BY

GREGORY A. THORNBURY

AND NED BUSTARD

In Christian art, the square halo identified a living person presumed to be a saint. Square Halo Books is devoted to publishing works that present contextually sensitive biblical studies and practical instruction consistent with the Doctrines of the Reformation. The goal of Square Halo Books is to provide materials useful for encouraging and equipping the saints.

First Edition 2015

Copyright ©2015 Square Halo Books
P.O. Box 18954, Baltimore, MD 21206
ISBN 978-1-941106-00-6
Library of Congress Control Number: 2015933142

CONTENTS

GOD THE FATHER GREGORY THORNBURY   I

BAPTISM CARTER STEPPER   II

TIME CHRISTIAN LEITHART   21

TRANSFORMATION SEAN GAFFNEY   31

EVIL JOSHUA LICKTER   43

SAVIOR TYLER HOWAT   53

INCARNATION CHRISTOPHER HANSEN   61

PRAYER NED BUSTARD   69

FAITH DAVID TALKS   79

SANCTITY OF LIFE REBEKAH HENDRIAN   93

TEMPTATION SARAH ETTER   99

SUFFERING J MARK BERTRAND   115

STORY MELODY GREEN   121

SCRIPTURE LEAH RABE   129

BIOS   135

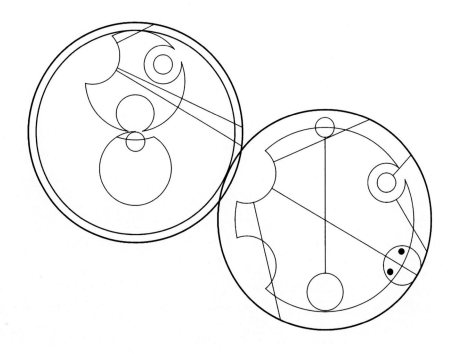

FOR THE T-BABES,
KATE AND CAROLYN,
FELLOW WHOVIANS
—GREG

FOR THE NYGUISTS—
IN HONOUR OF THE
FRIENDSHIP THAT GREW
FROM SHARING MUSIC,
FOOD, SCOTLAND,
CHRISTIANITY, AND
DOCTOR WHO
—NED

SPOILERS

THE DOCTOR: What's in that book?
RIVER: Spoilers.

We would like to take a moment at the beginning of this collection of essays to alert our readers about a potential danger in this book. *Bigger on the Inside: Christianity and Doctor Who* assumes that you have watched the *Doctor Who* series. Therefore, entire episodes—even seasons—are summarized, explained, and analyzed in these essays. All that to say, by all means keep reading. But for the record . . . *you were warned.*

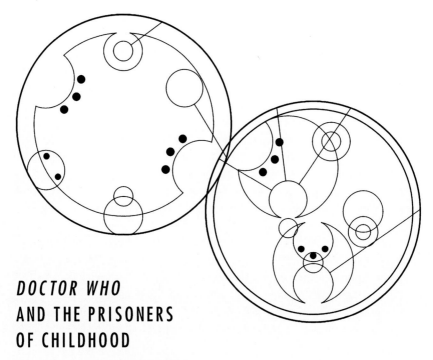

DOCTOR WHO
AND THE PRISONERS
OF CHILDHOOD

GOD THE FATHER: *Night Terrors*
ORIGINAL AIRDATE: SEPTEMBER 3, 2011

Why has *Doctor Who* operated so powerfully on the imagination of so many young people—young people who have become adults like me—for more than a half a century? Some might point to the growing popularity of the Sci-Fi genre in general for the better part of a century. That answer, bordering on being trivially true, cannot account for the phenomenon of a show that changes lead actors more often than Elton John switches sunglasses. No, Sci-Fi franchises come and go, but somehow *Who* keeps coming back. My guess is that this quirky show about a renegade Time Lord traveling through the past, present, and future in a 1960's British Police Box has this advantage: it operates on our oldest and most troubling emotions. That's why we keep coming back. That's why some of the most talented writers of this generation—Neil Gaiman, Mark Gatiss, and Steven Moffatt—have volunteered to write for and, in Moffatt's case, lead the show. We watch *Doctor Who* because it helps us get at the things that go psychoanalytic bump in the night.

As a way of getting at the heart of this peculiar genius that has spanned so many show writers over so many years, I entitled this chapter "*Doctor Who* and the Prisoners of Childhood" because I think the best way I have to pay homage to the spirit of Who is to make my reflections have the pretense of an episode.

Every year in my hometown, New York Comic Con attracts nearly two hundred thousand attendees. The event is bigger than almost any public mass gathering of which you can think in contemporary American society. The genre of comics, graphic novels, and fantasy possess a staying power that we carry with us through our lives. From the time I was five, I accompanied my father to the newsstand where I was allowed to choose from dozens of titles, the smell of ink and newsprint was nothing short of intoxicating. Ever since I can remember, the two dimensional world of comic books were my icons. Daredevil, The Dark Knight, and Spider Man were for me transcendental portals into the world of the hyper-real. When I moved to New York, I found an apartment on the twenty-eighth floor of a modern high rise on the West Side overlooking midtown. I'm sure part of the attraction involved my being able to step on out my balcony, close the door behind me, listen to the city, and think about Matt Murdock's grimacing upon reflection of the cruelty of The Kingpin. As much I liked the DC and Marvel Universes, nothing quite captured my imagination like *Who*.

I grew up watching *Doctor Who*, and the Doctor's regenerations were vivid markers in my childhood. For those unfamiliar with the show, the Doctor is able to survive mortal wounds by transitioning into another incarnation of the same person, with shared memories, but never the same personality. I first started watching the show on public television, starting with reruns of John Pertwee's Third Doctor, and then transitioning to Tom Baker's beloved portrayal of the Fourth. I invested in the mythology of the series. I learned as much as I could about the show. I read the novels and bought the comics. In sum, I was geeking out in the seventies

When the Fourth Doctor regenerated, it hit me as an eleven year old like a death in the family. But by the time Peter Davison's Fifth Doctor was finishing up his run in 1986, I was beginning to lose interest. I had a guitar, an amp, a driver's license, and a stack of LPs by The Clash, Elvis Costello, Squeeze, and early U2 to keep me distracted. Sure, I kept up with the show now and again, but it seemed to have lost its *élan* for me.

When *Doctor Who* relaunched in 2005, I found myself nostalgic once again for all things *Who*. I liked the quixotic portrayal of the character by Christopher Eccleston, but when David Tennant swaggered onto the screen as the Tenth Doctor, I, along with everyone else, was sold. The show became appointment television for the Thornbury family, and remains so to this day. With the likes of Russell T. Davies and Steven Moffatt respectively at the helm as head writer/ executive producer, the series regained its mythic dimensions for me. It didn't hurt matters when an apparently nearsighted but very nice lady stopped me on a street in London one day in 2009 and I asked if I could sign an autograph, thinking I might be Tennant.

Our girls shed big tears when the Doctor had to say goodbye to Rose on the beach of a lonely fjord in Norway. When the Tenth Doctor said his final words, "I don't want to go!" before he regenerated, we all cried in unison, "We don't want you to go!" But it wasn't long until Matt Smith's boyish Eleventh Doctor stole our hearts too. We shared the show in common with hundreds of under-grads with whom we found ourselves in community through the years. Then, on November 23, 2013, our whole family celebrated the 50th Anniversary of *Doctor Who* by going to see "The Day of the Doctor" in a theater in the Flatiron District who hundreds of other Whovians. My flight was late getting back into the city, so I found myself racing across the plaza at Lincoln Center to the sub-way station to make the train. Clad in a three piece tweed suit with a long scarf flapping in the wind, I heard a young woman call out sitting at the fountain, "Happy Anniversary, Doctor!" If ever I needed confirmation of my love for *Who* Culture, that was it.

Why do we love the Doctor? My simple answer is that he is every child's fan-tasy. Finding out *why* that is the case can be found by starting with psychologist Alice Miller's pathbreaking volume: *Prisoners of Childhood* or *The Drama of the Gifted Child*. Her thesis, simply put, asserts that children who spend their years attempting to compensate for the narcissistic needs of their mothers cannot, over time, bear the burden of being "good children."

Alice Miller's biography brought a unique gravitas to her work. She grew up in the shadow of National Socialism in the 1930's, and escaped the Jewish Ghetto in Piotkrów Trybulnalksi, was able to avoid to avoid detection living in Warsaw during the Nazi regime. Although she helped her mother and sister escape the ghetto, her father she could not save. He died in the ghetto in 1941.[1]

The extreme circumstances of her youth focused her on the vulnerability of children to all sorts of abuse. For Alice Miller, every child stood subject to the power of the adults in whose care they found themselves placed. She writes:

> But what does exist are children like this: intelligent, alert, attentive, extremely sensitive, and (because they are completely attuned to her well-being) entirely at the mother's disposal and ready for her use. Above all, they are transparent, clear, reliable, and easy to manipulate—as long as their true self (their emotional world) remains in the cellar of the transparent house in which they have to live —sometimes until puberty or until they come to analysis, and very often until they have become parents themselves.[2]

Think of the experience of Max in Spike Jonze's film adaptation of Maurice Sendak's *Where the Wild Things Are.* What is Max's day to day challenge? Managing the wide mood swings of Carol, the petulant Wild Thing. One has to give up one's life in order to keep those whom we love happy. Miller goes on to give a defining illustration of the conceit behind her thesis in *Prisoners of Childhood,* and I think it worthy to quote here at length.

In Alphonse Daudet's *Lettres de mon moulin* I have found a story that may sound rather bizarre, but nevertheless has much in common with what I have presented here. I shall summarize the story briefly.

Once upon a time there was a child who had a golden brain. His parents only discovered this by chance when he injured his head and gold instead of blood flowed out. They then began to look after him carefully and would not let him play with other children for fear of being robbed. When the boy was grown up and wanted to go out into the world, his mother said: "We have done so much for you, we ought to be able to share your wealth." Then her son took a large piece of gold out of his brain and gave it to his mother. He lived in great style with a friend who, however, robbed him one night and ran away. After that the man resolved to guard his secret and to go out to work, because his reserves were visibly dwindling. One day he fell in love with a beautiful girl who loved him too, but no more than the beautiful clothes he gave her so lavishly. He married her and was very happy, but after two years she died and he spent the rest of his wealth on her funeral, which had to be splendid. Once, as he was creeping through the streets, weak, poor, and unhappy, he saw a beautiful little pair of boots that would just have done for his wife. He forgot that she was dead—perhaps because his emptied brain no longer worked—and entered the shop to buy the boots. But in that very moment he fell, and the shopkeeper saw a dead man lying on the ground.

Daudet, who was to die from an illness of the spinal cord, wrote below the end of this story:

This story sounds as though it were invented, but it is true from beginning to end. There are people who have to pay for the smallest things in life with their very substance and their spinal cord. That is a constantly recurring pain, and then when they are tired of suffering.
Does not mother love belong to the "smallest," but also indispensable, things in life, for which many people paradoxically have to pay by giving up their living selves?[3]

In this story, as relayed by Miller via Daudet, I believe we find the key as to why we love the Doctor. Unlike other superhero stories, we don't know anything about his parents. The Doctor is the *eschatogeneis*—The last of the Time Lords, begotten, but eternal. Yes, he is the son of gods, incarnate on the earth. Even when we get a tantalizing bit about the Doctor's childhood, as we do in Steven Moffat's brilliant episode written for Peter Capaldi's Twelfth Doctor, *Listen*, we learn that the Doctor is something like an orphan. We hear people arguing in the poorly insulated shack in which he is forced to live as a child. Are these his parents? It does not seem so. These adults invite the boy to come back inside "with the other boys"—not his brothers. And so here is the takeaway: perhaps the Doctor has somehow escaped Miller's gifted child syndrome. Perhaps his greatest superpower is that he is free to discover his true self without having to reference any mother's (or Others) narcissistic cathexis. And what if that is the greatest fantasy of all, our secret desire, is to live life as a rebel Time Lord pursuing self awareness—all while taking out quite a few monsters to boot.

I think that it is worth mentioning in this connection—and sorry if there are spoilers for those of you who haven't gotten around yet to the Twelfth Doctor. If you have not, hurry up—Series 8 has some of the best writing that *Who* has had in years. For those who are not familiar with the characters, here seems to be a fundamental difference between the Eleventh Doctor, played originally by a then 27 year old Matt Smith, and the Twelfth Doctor, played by the 55 year old Peter Capaldi: The Eleventh Doctor played his character like an old man, a supremely self-confident, self-aware demigod, who at times seemed to just about have had it with saving human beings and the universe. One of the most memorable lines of dialogue for Smith's Doctor came as the Time Lord was comforting a little boy who was being terrorized by thoughts are of the re-emergence of an ancient reptilian race that had long been asleep deep beneath the earth: "Are you afraid of monsters?" the boy asks the Doctor. "No," the Time Lord responds, "monsters are afraid of me."[4]

The Twelfth Doctor seems positively childlike, struggling to discover what he wants to be when he grows up. Without any mother to define the issue for him, he asks his companion, Clara, whom he curiously refers to as his "carer," the following question: "Tell me, am I a good man?" Clara responds by opting out of Alice Miller's narcissistic mother syndrome, resisting to tell the Doctor that he is, in essence, "a good boy." Instead, she answers honestly, "I don't know." This theme reaches its culmination in the season finale of the Twelfth Doctor. For years, the series has obsessively asked itself and viewers, "Who is The Doctor?" The Doctor's enemies are keen to establish moral equivalence between them and the Time Lord. In "Death in Heaven," the Master[5] gives the "gift" of an army of Cybermen to the Doctor, based on the premise that only those who think that they are 'right' (i.e. righteous) should have an army to carry out their crusade. The Doctor clearly rejects the Master's overture, but is not sure why, until the following realization suddenly dawns on him:

> DOCTOR (to the Master): Thank you. Thank you so much. I really didn't know. I wasn't sure. You lose sight sometimes. Thank you! I am not a good man! And I'm not a bad man. I am not a hero. And I'm definitely not a president. And, no, I'm not an officer. Do you know what I am? I ... am ... an idiot, with a box and a screwdriver. Passing through, helping out, learning. I don't need an army, I never have, because I've got them (*Pointing to Danny and Clara*). Always them. Because love, it's not an emotion ... love is a promise.[6]

This is pure fantasy: discovering love. I think that *Doctor Who* is compelling to us subconsciously because, unlike other hero stories in fantasy literature, the Doctor doesn't have to reckon with his parents. And if the showrunners ever mess with this pretty consistent plot point going all of the way back to the original series, I will personally board a plane for Wales, and stage a hunger strike outside out of the BBC studios where the Sci-Fi series is filmed. This is what keeps *Who*, "Who."

Think about it. Every other hero is locked in an unhealthy relationship with the memory of his parents. Superman has to live up to the commission that he receives from his father Jor-El to guide the human race into an enlightened future. To everyone else, he's the Man of Steel. Inside his fortress of solitude, however, he's simply the "good son" who is trying to live up to the expectations of his parents.

Bruce Wayne is similar in this connection. Is he a demon or not? He'll never know if he's the good son because his parents were taken away from him. He is avenging his parents death, but when is enough enough? The Dark Knight will never know. The beat goes on in other Sci-Fi literature as well. Think of Ender in Orson Scott Card's famous novel. Ender is a "third" in military school. He is created to be self-sufficient and independent from his parents, but clearly he struggles with how to be stoic in the face of his responsibilities to family, nation-state, and religion.[7] And if I can be flippant for a moment, let me ask this question: weren't we all better off not knowing that Luke Skywalker's parents were Haydn Christensen and Natalie Portman? Weren't we better off without that particular origin story. Provenance kills.

I find the most terrifying narrative of all in this connection to be Harry Potter. He simultaneously has his parent's approval, but then again, he does not, either. His parents weakly smile at him and mutely convey that he's the good son through a desire mirror at Hogwart's when he is a young boy. The corporeal form of his patronus charm is the same as his father's: a stag. Is Harry receiving help from James? Or is he alone?

The Doctor, however, is startlingly different. He appeared to children on television in 1963 as a fully formed adult genius with long, white hair. The First Doctor, in fact, adopted the role of a grandfather. Children, who have always been the core audience of this often very scary show, always encounter the Doctor without any knowledge of his past. Even the children on the show, like Amelia Pond, greet him *in media res*, in the middle of the action. The Doctor has a frightening past, and most disturbing of all is the fact that he seems to have had very little guidance from any authority figures whatsoever on his way to becoming the defender of the universe. He is a rebel Time Lord, met *in media res*— in the middle of the action. When Rose Tyler meets the Ninth Doctor, the first words out of his mouth are pure adventure: "Hello, Rose Tyler. I'm the Doctor. Run for your life!" Rose runs so fast that she completely forgets for a time that her mother even exists. The Doctor is every girl and boy's dream.

What's interesting is that showrunner Steven Moffat has extended this fantasy to the female characters of the show during his run. In fact, as I think about it, it is a theme from the classic series as well. We knew almost nothing about the childhood of heroes like Sarah Jane and Leela. But Clara Oswald and Amy Pond are even more fascinating because we *know* they come from a dubious and uncertain provenance.

Amy meets the Doctor as a seven year old child. And although we are told she is living with her aunt, there is no explanation given for the missing parents. She is alone. Perhaps for this reason, from a psychological perspective, she is the only little girl in the world who is in a position to save the world. Undoubtedly, this is why that crack that is a tear in the fabric of the universe opened up next to her bed. The other Time Lords on Gallifrey, whom the Ninth and Tenth Doctor had assumed were completely gone and destroyed by the Daleks in the Time War, needed her help to mend the universe. One little girl without a mother.

Clara Oswald likewise inspires and perplexes the Doctor. He finds her on three different occasions in the history of the universe, the "impossible girl" who lives and dies, and keeps coming back. Whereas the Eleventh Doctor sees Clara as a mystery to be figured out, the Twelfth Doctor seems to see here through an obverse lens. Clara is the one whose supposed to be solving the mysteries of who the Doctor needs to be. Clara is forced to decide who should live and who should die, and how to get to the bottom of things that go bump in the night or crouch beneath our bed while we're asleep.

I like *Doctor Who* because there's very little out there in the world of Science Fiction that comes close to these themes of pure self-discovery. The closest thing so far I have found is Joe Kelly and J.M. Ken Niimura's heroine Barbara Thorson, the fifth grade girl portrayed in Image Comics 2010 limited run series, *I Kill Giants*. It's about a fifth grade girl who understands her life calling to be slaying giants. Her weapon of choice for the job is an ancient Norse war hammer, named Coveleski, which is hidden in her heart shaped purse.

As you might expect, Barbara has, you guessed it, no parents. Somewhere, she has a father, but he is not seen. She seems to live in some sort of children's home supervised by her sister. And so it's up to her to kill the giants herself, one little girl. And who are these monsters? Barbara explains to her school teacher, "A giant comes to a place and destroys everything in its path. Worse than that … it's not like a dumb hurricane or something. A giant is hate. It can't stand anything good, so smashing isn't enough. A giant comes to a place and takes everything from you. And when it's done, it's like, whatever made your life good was never there. And that's why giants have to die." The giants in this comic against which Barbara wages war are metaphorical. No father. No mother. Giants and a never ending parade of monsters being fought by a boy with no parents: this is the central plot device of *Doctor Who*.

It is my argument here that one of the many things that has made the mythology of the Doctor compelling to millions of people worldwide for more than five decades is that fulfills a fantasy of what our lives might look like if the fifth commandment were not a requirement for us. In a manner of speaking, then, the Character of the Doctor jockeys between themes of both Christ and antichrist. On the one hand, he is a dying and rising god who is perpetually suffering for the sins of the world. This is especially true of David Tennant's portrayal of the Tenth Doctor—who loves who human beings are but not what they do. Human beings are content to commit genocide (as in *The Christmas Invasion*) or to enslave an entire species such as the peace loving servile citizens of *The Planet of the Ood*. Still, the Doctor will never tire of defending the human race from alien threats.

But if what I am saying about the Doctor is true, he is also something of an antichrist because there is no Father for him to obey. He is alone in the universe without peer. This is both exciting and deeply troubling for the viewer. It is certainly the most interesting theme of Tennant's Doctor, which entertains this question: what happens when the Doctor goes "too far?" In *The Waters of Mars*, the Doctor alters the course of human history, changing the Time Stream of a key figure in history, to meet with the whims of his own conscience. Captain Adelaide Brooke, the principal figure involved, tells the Doctor, "The Doctor is wrong. The Time Lord victorious is wrong." Although the Doctor has saved her from certain death on a space exploration on Mars, a death she was supposed to die for the benefit of the human race, she commits suicide after the Doctor has safely brought her back home to *terra firma*. And all of the sudden, the Doctor is guilt stricken. "I've gone too far," we hear him say. It's clear that there's a higher standard of justice beyond him, but yet there is no one to whom he can pray, as Jesus does, "Father, let this cup pass from me. Nevertheless, not my will, but thine be done."

The thing that perhaps from a psychoanalytic perspective makes the Doctor a fantasy figure for us perhaps turns out to be the most terrible thought. If there is no love beyond the will to power, no transcendental authority, we are not only damned to carry a burden to transvalue all human values, but we must carry the burden alone. This horrible realization was too much for Nietzsche to bear, and it is true of Time Lords too. As much as some would like to believe that there is no Father to whom we can pray, sooner or later, even the Doctor will become weary of his own standard of justice.

All of these questions seem to have been exacerbated in Series 8 with the Twelfth Doctor. In *Into the Dalek*, the Doctor is forced for example to consider what it means to love your most hated enemy. What does it mean to confront doubts that you may not always know what is best for the people you love, when there is nothing like a word from God give you guidance on these matters?

Which brings us back to Alice Miller's *Prisoners of Childhood.* She considers the neuroses of children who have been manipulated by their parents to do things and be things that are not, if face, good in order to be "a good little boy" or a "good little girl." Certainly this is the fate of too many children in modern society. What would it be like to see an alternative—a covenant community in which parents see themselves not as narcissistic arbiters of behavior, but legatees of tradition that protects and promotes the flourishing of children? But this very much is something, thankfully, that Matt Smith's Eleventh Doctor gets to see. One of my favorite examples of this is an episode entitled *Night Terrors*—which deals with the theological theme of what it means to be adopted as sons. It deals with the nightmares of a little boy named George who through a perception filter is able to lock his fears away in his wardrobe. It's Narnia's wardrobe in reverse. Now it also just so happens that George is an alien child, who has found his way to earth in order to be the son of a mom and a dad who cannot have children. Inside the wardrobe are crude and creepy looking dolls, who desperately want someone with whom to play. As the Doctor's companions quickly learn when they get sucked into the wardrobe, when the Dolls grab a hold of you to play with you, you turn into a lifeless and soulless toy like them too. In the end, the Doctor realizes that the only way for George to confront his fears and to stop the advance of the killer playthings is to accept the love of his adoptive father. Once he does, all is right with the world.

It is a reminder that the best gift we can give to the Doctor, and our own children, is the sacrifice love of a father and mother. We also can point those prisoners of childhood to the baptism of Jesus, the beloved son in whom the Father is well-pleased. He is loved, and he loves us. And there is nothing more that we can do to earn this extravagant gesture of grace.

Still, there are signs that despite his self-imposed narrative that he is alone in the universe, with a very cynical attitude toward transcendent possibilities, the Twelfth Doctor finds himself wanting to believe in grace and something "coming from the outside"—despite himself. In *Mummy on the Orient Express*, we hear the Doctor say, "I know a lot [of mythology], because from time to time, it turns out to be true." What sorts of myths is he open to reconsidering? We find a clue in *The Last Christmas*. When one of the scientists (the shop girl) aboard the expedition confronting the Dream Crabs protests, "What? You're asking Santa for help? He doesn't exist!" The Doctor responds, "And how would you know that? How did you become an expert on what does and doesn't exist?" Indeed, it's something that reason tells us that doesn't exist—a myth for whom Santa serves as the stand-in—that awakens both the Doctor and Clara from the sleep of death and restores both of them to new life; the Doctor receives Clara back from near death. As they race to the TARDIS for new adventures, Clara enthuses to the Doctor: "Look at you, all happy! That's rare." "You know what's rarer?" he replies, "Second chances. I never get a second chance, so what happened this time? I don't even know who to thank."

Sitting at home next to the Christmas tree, finishing this episode, I felt myself wanting to tell the Doctor: "Who to thank? Ah, that. He's your heavenly Father. You know, sometimes myths actually do turn out to be true."

ENDNOTES

1   Martin Miller, Das wahre "Drama des begabten Kindes", *Die Tragödie Alice Miller* Freiburg im Breisgau: Kreuz Verlag. 2013, 26–44; cited from "Miller, Alice," http://en.m.wikipedia.org/wiki/Alice_Miller_(psychologist).

2   Alice Miller, *Prisoners of Childhood; or, The Drama of the Gifted Child* (New York: Basic Books, 1981); *Das Drama des Begabten Kindes,* trans. Ruth Ward, 28.

3   Ibid., 28-29.

4   Chris Chibnall, "The Hungry Earth," *Doctor Who,* Season 5, Episode 8, May 22, 2010.

5   The Master is a renegade Time Lord and the Doctor's arch-enemy. He has been described as "one of the most evil and corrupt beings [the] Time Lord race [had] ever produced" (*The Five Doctors*). The Master returned in Series 8, inexplicably regenerated into a female body. As such, he changed his name to "the Mistress"—or Missy, for short.

6   Stephen Moffat, "Death in Heaven," *Doctor Who,* Series 8, Episode 12, November 8, 2014.

7   Orson Scott Card, *Ender's Game* (New York: Tor Science Fiction, 1985; reprint 1994).

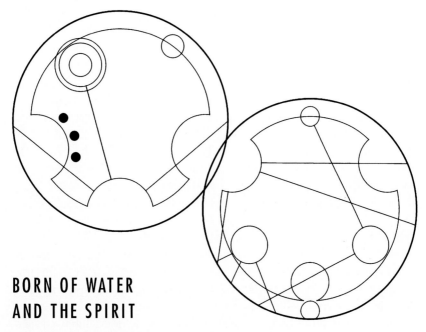

BORN OF WATER AND THE SPIRIT

BAPTISM: *Journey's End*
ORIGINAL AIRDATE: JULY 5 2008

We are defined by our stories. In each stage of our lives, there are marked moments where we can perceive with clarity how our lives have changed, shaping our individual identities in unique ways. But we often feel as if our lives are incomplete or insufficient, somehow a bit too drab and boring for anyone to really notice. In rebellion to this, we want to believe that a greater adventure is occurring. We want to be a part of something important, and we want to believe that some great plan is unfolding, a story that explains the universe to us. As C.K. Robertson puts it, speaking of our need for superheroes and their stories, "The great myths of the ancient world provided for human beings lenses of imagination through which to see and understand—and relate to—their universe,"[1] and such a need has not left the human race. In short, we want our story to collide with a grander, more important story, so that we might be swept up in a great adventure, that we might somehow become important, even if just for a moment.

THE BIG PICTURE

Is there a greater story out there, a grand narrative of which we humans might take part? Or is it only possible in the fantastic world of time traveling aliens with two hearts? I encountered *Doctor Who* a couple years into the reboot series, and at first I was skeptical. As an Anglophile who enjoys wacky antics, I was willing to give it a shot. But as I watched I discovered that, like the best science fiction, the show engaged with interesting and important ideas. It strikes me that part of the appeal of *Doctor Who* is that it reflects the reality mentioned above: that we human beings find our existence a bit drab, but that sometimes someone might be lucky enough to be caught up into an adventure that changes our lives forever. Normal, everyday, mildly boring people are pulled into the Doctor's adventures, and in the process become heroes in their own right. The viewer is invited to join their growth and development as they, following the Doctor, are transformed into people of great deeds and heroic character.

While reflecting on how to write this essay, I realized first that any comparison to serious Christian theology might come off as a bit stretched. And yet, I realized secondly, that the deep yearning to be part of something more, and to believe that great things happen in the universe, is acknowledged and answered by both subjects of this book: *Doctor Who,* and the Christian faith. In this way, *Doctor Who* serves, as C.S. Lewis remarked once, as a "real though unfocused gleam of divine truth falling upon human imagination."[2] The popularity of *Doctor Who* reflects this basic desire of the human soul for meaning and value in a universe that seems meaningless and arbitrary. A reflection on *Doctor Who,* therefore, can help us examine more carefully, and appreciate more fully, the important aspects of our faith.

"It's bigger on the inside." These words mark a new moment in the lives of those known as "Companions," the lucky few whose otherwise ho-hum lives happen to cross paths with the whirlwind life of that most enigmatic of characters, Doctor Who.[3] These words are spoken on first entering the TARDIS by various characters who choose (or are chosen) to accompany the Doctor. Rose Tyler, Mickey Smith, Donna Noble, Sarah Jane Smith, Wilfred Mott, and Amy Pond—these are just some of the names of those whose lives are irrevocably changed by crossing the threshold of the TARDIS and the uttering of those words. When they speak those words, and take that step, they are also choosing to follow the Doctor. They are becoming a part of something bigger. They are a part of saving a world or the universe from annihilation, or sometimes, even just a person or two. The grand story that is the Doctor's life, soaring through space and time with a desire to do mercy, help those in need, and face evil is now their life, too.

In the real world it is generally thought that such opportunities do not come to so called normal people. For us, it's just work, diapers, holiday gatherings, and catching some telly before bed. It doesn't seem like there is any great story, any grand narrative of defeating evil or rescuing the helpless. The Christian faith denies this view of the world, surrendering to our bland fates with a shrug and a sigh. For Christians, there is a story that began a long time ago, and continues to this day. It awaits the final, definitive moment of triumph; but in the meantime, those who believe it press on with confidence. This is the story of God's victory in the world, through Jesus Christ's life, death, resurrection, ascension, intercession, and (eventual) return. Between the ascension and the return of Jesus, Christians take part in the work of Christ, telling the world about His work and showing His kindness to them.

Before any of that can happen, however, we have to cross our own "threshold." Companions are marked by entering the Doctor's TARDIS, and by re-marking on the remarkable fact that it is, indeed, bigger on the inside. For the Christian, that threshold is baptism. This is the initiation of the Christian into the Church, a moment where a person is marked, and from that moment transformed, becoming a member of this mission of God. Sacraments (Baptism and the Lord's Supper) serve a purpose in the Church often forgotten, or misunderstood. As we started by pointing out, certain marked moments define a person; and sacraments serve as these marked moments in the Christian life. But it is more than simply having a memory of some commitment we made once upon a time. The sacraments are actually vehicles of divine grace, simple things that communicate something mysterious and powerful to us. They are "not only badges or tokens of Christian men's profession, but . . . sure witnesses, and effectual signs of grace . . . by the which he doth work invisibly in us."[4] A sacrament is therefore a simple sign, but also a vehicle of grace, a medium by which God communicates His power and love to His people. Much in the same way, what appears to be a strangely dressed man with a police box makes the Companions something other than what they were. By receiving baptism, the Christian receives grace by the Holy Spirit, and is initiated into the work of God.

Romans 6:1–11 fleshes out this idea in vivid detail. Vss. 2–5 read,

> Do you not know that all of us who have been baptized into Christ Jesus were baptized into his death? We were buried therefore with him by baptism into death, in order that, just as Christ was raised from the dead by the glory of the Father, we too might walk in newness of life. For if we have been united with him in a death life his, we shall certainly be united with him in a resurrection like his.

A person is thus united to Christ, and so shares in His great acts. We don't just join a club; we are joined to Christ, and we make a commitment that could cost us. Our identity has changed in that moment, and it is not possible for us to go back to the same-old-same-old afterwards. Likewise, when a person enters into this adventure with the Doctor, they embrace the danger and excitement, and are forever transformed by that experience. As one Christian creed puts it, "Baptism is not only a sign of profession, and mark of difference, whereby Christian men are discerned from others that be not christened, but it is also a sign of Regeneration or New-Birth, whereby, as by an instrument, they that receive Baptism rightly are grafted into the Church. . . "[5] Water makes us new people, by the operation of a force greater and more mysterious than we can fathom. In the world of *Doctor Who*, it is the step into the TARDIS that serves as an entry into the new world.

When the Christian receives this baptism, they (or their parents in the case of infants) also proclaim their faith. There is a response to baptism to indicate that what is being offered there is understood and received. Usually this is the form of a creed such as the Apostle's Creed, whose roots lie in an early Christian baptismal vow. The profession of a creed is acknowledgment that the person baptized is entering a strange, mysterious reality for which only a kind of stunned reverence will do, a response that really only has a sliver of real understanding. "I believe . . . " Christians have said for millennia. "It's bigger on the inside," says the Companions. They may not understand it, but they know it to be true, and it is thus acknowledged that they have entered into something for which no further explanation is possible.

The fundamental nature of this initiation is grace. Christians cannot baptize themselves, and in the historical traditions, it is normally done by ordained ministers acting in the name of Christ. Ultimately, it is God who is baptizing us with His Spirit, as His "sacraments are not contingent upon the moral character of the celebrant but depend on God alone. Humans are freed from the need to make the sacrament happen; only God can do that."[6] When the Doctor desires a new Companion, it is *he* who asks *them* if they want to join him. He comes seemingly out of nowhere, into their lives, to rescue them from some impending doom, and then invites them to journey with him. They must respond, undoubtedly; but the initiative lies with the Doctor.

WHAT DOES IT MEAN TO ENTER THIS STORY?

Baptism is all well and good, one might say. But how does this fit into *Doctor Who*? Besides the fact that there is a regular sort of initiation involved, is there really anything to learn from all this? I believe there is. Remember, we all love stories, and "Myths inspire the realization of the possibility of your perfection."[7] We want to be a part of this wonderful narrative. But there is always a first step, whether baptism or walking through the door of a big blue box. When that happens, as I spoke of above, something changes. The identity of the person changes irrevocably, transforming them in a fundamental way.

This point is heavily emphasized in the Series 4 finale of the reboot series,

"Journey's End." In this episode, the second of two parts, the Doctor is facing one of his oldest enemies, Davros, the creator of the Daleks. But of course, he is not alone. Friends start to show up to help him, friends from every conceivable corner—mostly Companions—some old, some new. The Earth has been stolen, and even the Doctor can't find it. It has been placed into formation with 26 other planetary bodies, hidden away in a time pocket, to create what Davros calls a "reality bomb" that will destroy, well, all of reality. The Doctor and Donna Noble are desperately trying to find Earth, while a handful of former Companions on Earth are working to send him a signal. They succeed in this, leading the Doctor to the time pocket where Earth has been hidden.

"Look at all you, you clever people," the Doctor exclaims. Martha Jones and Jack Harkness are there, only recently departed from the TARDIS. Sarah Jane Smith is there with K-9.[8] Even Mickey Smith, Jackie Tyler, and most importantly of all, Rose Tyler are there as well, from an alternate universe (no small feat of transportation in itself). They are all there, fighting to bring the Doctor to Earth, and prepared to die for him. They have all been marked as Companions, and though they are now in different places, with unique missions of their own, they are all ultimately committed to the Doctor, and to his leadership. They are his people.

To bring the Doctor, however, requires an enormous sacrifice. Harriet Jones, former Prime Minister[9] and a follower of the Doctor, orchestrates the beacon that summons both he and Donna. She is tracked down by the Daleks and killed. But it won't stop there. "The Children of Time will gather," intones the rather creepy, insane Dalek Caan, "and one of them will die." Following the Doctor is a dangerous proposition. He has a mission, however ambiguous, to defend good and root out evil, and to enforce justice and peace. These are not principles that can be enforced without opposition and conflict. The Doctor has the fortune of being able to regenerate, at least a certain number of times. But his Companions do not. When they fall, they stay that way, and for all of his power, he cannot raise them from the dead.

The Doctor and his people are caught in a stand-off with Davros. Jack and Sarah Jane clutch a warp star, a "warpfold conjugation trapped in a carbonized shell... an explosion... An explosion waiting to happen," as Jack tells Mickey, ready to make that explosion happen if necessary. Meanwhile, Martha Jones has used the Osterhagen key, which activates a string of nuclear warheads around the world that will detonate at her command. These Companions are all ready, all committed to destroy themselves—and even Earth—if it means stopping Davros. Davros, addressing the Doctor says, "But this is the truth, Doctor. You take ordinary people and you fashion them into weapons... Already I have seen them sacrifice today, for their beloved Doctor," referencing Harriet Jones.

"How many more? Just think. How many have died in your name?" Davros continues to grind into the Doctor, pointing out the devotion and almost fanatical commitment of the Doctor's friends to him.

The Doctor's response, "They're just trying to help," comes off a bit lame, frankly. In the episode, or the series more generally, there really never is a satisfactory answer to the accusation that the Doctor leaves a swath of destruction behind him. But what is interesting here is not the weakness or fallibility of the Doctor; no, what is interesting and compelling is the truly enormous lengths his Companions will go to in order to aid his mission. Crossing boundaries between universes, in the case of Rose, Mickey, and Jackie. All facing death, and even willing to destroy their own planet if it will save the universe. And throughout the series, the sacrifices they make are not superficial. Rose, Mickey, and Jackie are taken from this universe to another; Martha's unrequited love goes unreturned; Captain Jack dies;[10] later, Rory Williams waits 2,000 years so he can save his love; Amy Pond and he are both victims of the Weeping Angels; and Donna perhaps has the worst fate of all, having to have her memories wiped, taking from her what made her special: her time with the Doctor. Yet through all of this, they all remain committed to him.

The episode resolves with bitter-sweetness. Davros is defeated, but as he and the Daleks are destroyed, the mad seer Dalek Caan utters, "One will still die." Like most prophecies, this one is cryptic, but we find out soon enough what is meant. In the previous episode, the Doctor had been shot by the Daleks. He regenerated just enough to heal his body, but then channeled his remaining regenerative energy into his own severed hand.[11] This creates a second Doctor, but in the process of this creation, Donna touches him. An exchange occurs between them, making this second Doctor Time Lord with a bit of human, and Donna human with a bit of Time Lord. This pairing is ultimately what allows them to defeat Davros; while the two Doctors distract the Daleks, Donna is able to use her Time Lord knowledge to unobtrusively defeat them.

But that power (and that gift) come with an enormous cost. After their victory, Donna begins to fall apart. Her mind cannot contain the enormity of the Time Lord mind. If she continues in this state, she will "burn up," as the Doctor puts it. He is forced to remove all of her memories, all of the joy and wonder she experiences while traveling with him. In a very real sense, that Donna, the one who was changed by the Doctor, dies.

Yes, the Companions sacrifice much. But why shouldn't they? That is what happens when a person is swept up into a great story, an adventure, and a purpose that is greater than themselves. When they step into the TARDIS, and say those words, "it's bigger on the inside," they become new people, and will always bear the marks of that moment. They sacrifice much because the Doctor has sacrificed much on their behalf. They sacrifice much because the Doctor has chosen to include them in his great (if somewhat ambiguous) mission. They sacrifice much because it is better to suffer and die serving a great cause than to wither away caring only for TV and gossip.

This is the Christian story. When an event changes us in such a way, it begins to determine how we will respond to future situations. Who we are determines what we do, in large part; a will strengthened by adversity will overcome obstacle, or a traumatic experience may make us weak in the face of our fear. In the face of adversity, conflict, and evil, how will we respond? To what will we turn to for strength? What life-shaping events will carry us through, whole? In the earliest years of Christianity, martyrdom spoke in ways that the most eloquent words could not, turning those martyrs into "intelligible utterances of God."[12] They sacrificed enormously—unto death—because their savior did so for them. Soldiers of peace, they did not succumb to evil, or step away once it got too hard, but embraced the opportunity to be like the One who invited them into this story. "Eighty and six years have I served Him," Bishop Polycarp of Smyrna is reported to have said, "and He has done me no wrong. How then can I blaspheme my King and my Savior?"[13] The difference is in the savior. Whereas the Doctor is as broken and often as fallible as his Companions are, and routinely does hurt them, Jesus Christ does not. His people are hurt, they suffer, and face evil; but these things are not due to His weakness, or inability, or thoughtlessness. They occur to make us more than what we are, to re-create us in the Image of Christ. And whereas it is only the Doctor who can regenerate when Death knocks on the door, we, who share in Christ, united to Him in death, are also united to Him in resurrection. We also rise to new life, eternal life, when time comes to an end.

Does this mean that baptism guarantees the same result with each person who receives it? Will all be willing to sacrifice, to suffer, and to die for their leader? This thorny question has been much debated. Suffice to say, while it is approached differently by different traditions, they typically all recognize that however powerful these divine acts are, they can ultimately prove fruitless. As one catechism answer puts it, "I am born a sinner by nature, separated from God, but in baptism, *rightly received*, I am made God's child by grace through faith in Christ."[14] (Emphasis mine) To rightly receive baptism is to respond in faith, to reflect in one's life the grace that baptism communicates. In Matthew 13:3–8, Jesus tells the famous Parable of the Sower. Here we see that the grace of the Gospel is spread about widely, but not all respond as they should; some were the hard ground of the path, some rocky ground where they could not take root, and some were choked by thorns. The faith of these "seeds" perished, while only the seeds that fell upon good soil grew.

And so it is with the good Doctor. We tend to remember the Companions that stick around: Rose, Donna, Amy; but what about those who don't? Adam Mitchell was a short-lived Companion of the Ninth Doctor, appearing in only two episodes.[15] He is taken on board the TARDIS as a Companion, but in the very next episode, betrays the Doctor's trust by using advanced technology to send information back to his own time for his own gain. "The whole of history could have changed because of you," the Doctor tells him. Adam replies, pleadingly, "I just wanted to help!" "You were helping yourself," comes the honest and harsh reply, before he is summarily dumped out of the TARDIS. A legitimate Companion he was, but when a moral challenge presented itself, he showed himself to be shallow soil. Grace might be offered, and a chance at joining a glorious adventure, but it has to be received. Martha was arguably only ever a Companion because of an attraction to the Doctor, i.e. for the wrong reasons. Mickey always seemed to struggle as a Companion, especially as it drew him and Rose apart. And initially, Donna wanted to join the Doctor, but said no.[16] Not all Companions start or end the same way.

Everyone responds a bit differently to the invitation into a great story. Some don't live out the reality that their initiation represents, and are just in it for the fame, the money, or for romance. Some just aren't ready to commit yet, and some will always struggle with it. But the invitation is there, and the story goes on one way or the other. We may never have a chance to join an alien Doctor on escapades through time and space, but we have received an invitation into an even greater story, that we enter by the Water and the Word, by a step and a statement. And once we step inside this magnificent story, we too will find ourselves exclaiming that "it's bigger on the inside!"

ENDNOTES

1   C.K. Robertson, "Sorcerers and Supermen: Old Mythologies in New Guises," in *Religion and Science Fiction*, ed. James McGrath (Pickwick Publications, 2011, Eugene, OR), 33.

2   Robertson, "Sorcerers and Supermen," 33.

3   This statement appears most consistently in the reboot series, but occurring as far back as the Third Doctor.

4   39 Articles of Religion, Article 25, "The Book of Common Prayer" (The Church Hymnal Corporation, New York, 1979), 872.

5   "Book of Common Prayer," 873.

6   James F. White, "Introduction to Christian Worship," Third Edition (Abingdon Press, Nashville, TN 2000), 196.

7   Robertson, "Sorcerers and Supermen," 56.

8   Both Companions from the original run of the series. Though technically, it was the Mark IV version of K-9, not the K-9 first given to the Fourth Doctor. Sarah Jane was an investigative journalist who traveled with the Third and Fourth Doctors. At the time of this episode she was defending Earth in *The Sarah Jane Adventures*.

9   "Yes, we know who you are."

10   Though to be fair, this happens a lot and never quite sticks.
11   "The Christmas Invasion."
12   Saint Ignatius of Antioch, "The Epistle to the Romans," in *Early Christian Writings*, trans. Maxwell Staniforth (Dorset Press, 1986), pg. 104.
13   "Martyrdom of Polycarp," Staniforth, 158-159.
14   "To Be A Christian: An Anglican Catechism." ACNA Catechesis Task Force, 2014. Pg. 30.
15   "Dalek" and "The Long Game."
16   See "Runaway Bride, series 3; Donna doesn't join him until the beginning of series 4.

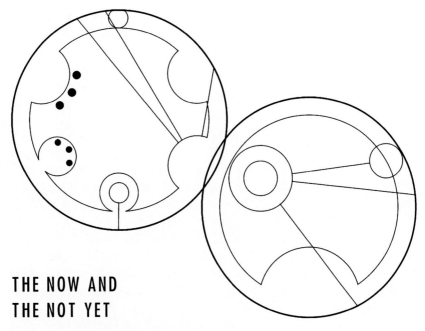

THE NOW AND
THE NOT YET

TIME: *The Wedding of River Song*
ORIGINAL AIRDATE: OCTOBER I, 2011

> Time present and time past
> Are both perhaps present in time future,
> And time future contained in time past.
> If all time is eternally present
> All time is unredeemable.
> —T. S. Eliot, *Four Quartets: Burnt Norton*

According to Samuel Alexander, the 20th century marked the beginning of a period where time took a place in the spotlight.

> I do not mean that we have waited until today to become familiar with Time; I mean that we have only just begun, in our speculation, to take Time seriously, and to realize that in some way or other Time is an essential ingredient in the constitution of things.[1]

Alexander is a little modern for my taste. I think he misses the incredible richness of the Biblical view of Time, reflected in some parts of Christian art and culture (especially during the medieval period). He does make an interesting point, however, in drawing attention to our culture's current fascination with Time. In the last one hundred years, science fiction has blossomed in novels, movies, radio plays, video games, and TV shows. If there's one defining quality of Sci-Fi, it is the genre's playful fascination with this idea of Time, either in the form of alternate histories, speculative futures, intergalactic exploration, or the old, ever-tantalizing standby: time travel.

The irony of attempting a history of time travel is not lost on me, so I will wrinkle the fabric of history and jump forward to everyone's favorite show about an affable Doctor and his incredible blue police box. *Doctor Who* is an anomaly on TV, a befuddling collection of stories about a character so vast in personality that it takes over a dozen actors to portray him in the television series alone. The topics and themes explored in the show cover everything from friendship to immortality to fashion and beyond. But time travel is the one thing that's present in every *Doctor Who* episode. And perhaps it is the reason I, and millions of others, find ourselves drawn to the show. And who can blame us? The appeal of the Doctor popping out of the TARDIS in the middle of sixteenth century England, waving his sonic screwdriver, never gets old.

In addition to teaching lessons about loyalty, honor, and sacrifice, *Doctor Who* has a lot to say about Time itself. The Doctor has a pretty cavalier attitude towards Time, except in certain moments when there's a risk of "crossing time streams" or "rewriting fixed points." Despite his easygoing attitude, even the Doctor realizes that there are certain boundaries in Time that cannot—or must not—be crossed. God does not enter into the *Doctor Who* universe very often. We're not told where the laws that govern this universe came from, but they clearly include some kind of fixed sequence of events, a "primary timeline" of sorts. As the Doctor spins through the corridors of Time in the TARDIS, he's free to pursue adventure wherever it lies, as long as he doesn't create paradoxes that would tear the world apart. As strange as it sounds, I think the adventures of the Doctor may help us better understand Time in our world, and thereby, its Creator.

At this point, our conversation about Time is starting to get a bit abstract, so let me try to reattach it to the real world. In our world, how do we relate to Time? And how does God relate to Time, and to us within it?

Most of us probably imagine Time as a filmstrip, or perhaps a book. We experience events from beginning to end, not skipping forwards and backwards from place to place. The common Christian view puts God outside Time, flipping through the pages of reality as though it were placed in front of Him like a book. At any moment, in past, present, or future, He is able to work His will in the world. As the medieval philosopher Boethius stated, God "grasps and possesses simultaneously the entire fullness of an unchanging life, a life which lacks nothing of the future and has lost nothing of the changing past." To God, the "infinity of changing time" is as "one present before him."[2] C. S. Lewis agreed: "God, I believe, does not live in a Time-series at all. His life is not dribbled out moment by moment like ours: with Him it is still 1920 and already 1960."[3]

Boethius and Lewis both knew that God is less than God if He does not know what the future holds. The God of Abraham, Isaac, and Jacob is the One who knows the beginning and the end. He is the Alpha and the Omega. With Him, a thousand years are like a day, and a day is like a thousand years (2 Pet. 3:8). Clearly, God is outside of Time in some sense, and we rightly may derive comfort from that fact. Our eternal Father is not subject to the pressures of Time, so He can coolly and competently solve the problems that we fret over. How silly we must look from His perspective, worrying about what the day will bring. Don't we know that His mercies are new every morning (Lam 3:23)?

The trouble is, God also exists in Time. He does not merely dabble in it as though it were a paddling pool. Read the Old Testament and you will find again and again that God identifies Himself with actions and events occurring in Time. In the beginning (a moment in Time) He created the heavens and the earth (Gen. 1:1). He brought the children of Israel out of bondage in Egypt and continually reminds them of it (Ex. 20:2, Ps. 81:10, Hosea 13:4). He dwells in the tabernacle, and later in the temple, in the form of a glorious cloud that rubbernecking Israelites could actually gawk at (Ex. 40:34, 1 Kg. 8:11). He brings up His past actions as a testimony to His power and faithfulness and He makes promises that He plans to uphold (Deut. 31:6, Hos. 11:1). God does uphold the past, so it does not collapse into nothingness, but that's hardly the same thing as combining past and present into one atemporal Moment.

Far be it from me to deny that God is eternal. The Bible is quite clear on that fact. William Lane Craig summarizes it nicely:

> The Bible teaches clearly that God is eternal. Isaiah proclaims God as "the high and lofty One who inhabits eternity" (Isa. 57:15). In contrast to the pagan deities of Israel's neighbors, the Lord never came into existence nor will He ever cease to exist. As the Creator of the universe, He was there in the beginning, and He will be there at the end. "I, the Lord, the first, and with the last; I am He" (Isa. 41:4).[4]

God has no beginning and no end. So when God describes His own past and future, is He simply speaking of Himself in terms that we are familiar with? Or is there some sense in which eternality does not equal timelessness? Instead of saying that God is outside and apart from Time, it is far better to say that God revels in Time. We will get to the distinction in a moment, and the Doctor may help us understand.

In the Incarnation, God identifies Himself both in and with Time. A specific day and hour on Earth marks the birth of Jesus. Jesus lived on Earth a certain number of days and ascended into heaven a certain number of years ago. The many genealogies in the Bible are profound examples of God's providence and love for His people because they locate His people in Time. In a sense, God is outside of Time, but in another sense, He has chosen to reveal Himself in Time. Lewis says that, "God has no history. He is too completely and utterly real to have one."[5] I agree with the point Lewis is trying to make, but I quibble with his terms. God *does* have a history. He has chosen a history for Himself, which we find in the Bible.

If God identifies Himself with temporal events, what does that mean for Time? It means that Time is not something that God wants us to escape from, because Time is not inherently bad. Just like everything else, Time must be redeemed (Eph. 5:16). We can already see something of what redeemed Time might look like, since our experience of Time tells us something about who God is.

If Time did not temper our progress, we would be overwhelmed by the reality that God created. "Time is what keeps everything from happening at once," as Ray Cummings once said, and it is also what keeps us from being submerged in eternity. As T. S. Eliot says, "Humankind cannot bear very much reality."[6] We are limited by the boundaries of our physical bodies, but God is omnipresent. We are limited temporally, while God is eternal. God is not timeless. It's far better to think of Him as having an overabundance of Time. He fills it as completely as He fills space. In His Wisdom, He carefully administers it in doses small enough for us to drink.

Now that everyone is well and truly muddled, the Doctor will swoop in and help me elucidate. In "The Wedding of River Song," the Doctor gives us an entry point into understanding how God can be both inside and outside of time, and why timelessness might not be the best way to think of His Triune life.

"The Wedding of River Song" is the thirteenth and final episode of the sixth series of *Doctor Who*. Written by Steven Moffat, the plot revolves around the death of the Doctor and his friendship with Rory Williams, Amelia Pond, and River Song.

Of the show's many forays into the paradoxes of time travel, few are so complicated as the Doctor's relationship to River Song.[7] The Doctor first meets River in *Silence in the Library*, when she arrives unannounced and reveals that she knows everything about him, including his name, which he has told to (almost) no one. As the Doctor says, "There's only one reason I would ever tell anyone my name. There's only one time I could."[8] River proceeds to sacrifice herself to save those trapped in the computer system in the Library. The Doctor is able to save her at the last moment, preserving her consciousness in a computer, but he does not have time to find out how she knows what she knows.

Over the next few seasons, more and more information about River Song is revealed. As it turns out, she has been living her life in a frenzy of time-traveling, with the result that she and the Doctor "never meet in the right order."[9] As River expresses it, "We were living our lives in the wrong order, the Doctor and me. And in all our future meetings, I would know him more and he would know me less."[10] We will focus on one adventure that they shared: the time the Doctor died, or more accurately, the time he didn't.

In *The Impossible Astronaut*, an astronaut rises from the still waters of Lake Silencio in Utah and shoots the Doctor while he's having a picnic with his friends. Later in Series 6, in *The Wedding of River Song*, we see the same story unfold differently. This time, we discover that the astronaut is River Song, but as she rises from the lake, she refuses to kill the Doctor. As a result, all of Time collapses on itself, and all of history begins to happen at once. As we've already discussed, there are certain events in the *Doctor Who* universe, "fixed points in Time," which provide a sort of graph upon which the rest of Time hangs. In one of the most well known and well loved phrases from the *Doctor Who* canon, the Tenth Doctor explains, "People assume that time is a strict progression of cause to effect. But actually from a non-linear, non-subjective viewpoint it's more like a big ball of wibbly-wobbly timey-wimey ... stuff ... "[11] But even the wibbles and the wobbles need a place to hang their hat. These fixed points give the universe its shape.

The trouble comes when one of the fixed points (the death of the Doctor) is manipulated by River Song, wearing the astronaut suit. Of her own free will, she refuses to kill the Doctor, creating the temporal anomaly. All of history happens at once, and it does so in a way that is delightfully *Doctor Who*. In this bizarro world, Winston Churchill is the Holy Roman Emperor, living in Buckingham Palace, while outside, signs warn Londoners not to feed the pterodactyls and Roman chariots wait at stoplights. Every clock is stuck at 5:02 in the afternoon, and when Churchill wonders about the oddity of it, he and his physician have the following conversation:

CHURCHILL: What time do you have, doctor?
MALOHKEH: Two minutes past five, Caesar.
CHURCHILL: It's always two minutes past five. Day or night, it's always two minutes past five in the afternoon. Why is that?
MALOHKEH: Because that is the time, Caesar.
CHURCHILL: And the date. It's always the twenty second of April. Does it not bother you?
MALOHKEH: The date and the time have always been the same, Caesar.

Why should it start bothering me now?

Many notice that Time seems to have stopped, but no one's quite sure what to do about it. No one can remember any history. As far as they're concerned, Time has always been stopped. Finally, Churchill calls for the soothsayer, who turns out to be the Eleventh Doctor sporting a beard and a shabby toga. "Explain to me in terms that I can understand what happened to time," commands Emperor Churchill and the Doctor responds, "A woman."

This episode is part of a larger arc that covers the entire season, and more. The plot is punishingly complex, but the important part is this: unless the Doctor dies, at the precise moment he was meant to at Lake Silencio, Time will not merely cease to move, it will begin to disintegrate as it becomes increasingly unstable. The Doctor tells River, "Time isn't just frozen, it's disintegrating. It will spread and spread and all of reality will simply fall apart."

In its own whimsical, Whovian way, this episode gives us hints of what a timeless world might look like. Apart from silly, fun details like Winston Churchill lecturing the Doctor about digital downloads, life in this world begins to be more and more uncertain. How can anyone or anything be reliable when the past and the future have ceased to exist and there is no Time but the present? At one point, Churchill sniffs the air and says, "Gunsmoke!" Then raising his revolver, he adds with evident surprise, "Oh, I appear to have fired this."

As the Doctor struggles to convey the seriousness of the temporal disaster to a baffled Winston Churchill, the villains of the story appear. They are creatures called the Silence,[12] a religious organization of mysterious intent who want the Doctor to die, or at least, do not want him to remain alive. Their most dastardly quality is their ability to affect the memories of those who come into contact with them. In order to remember the Silence, you must always keep them in your sight. Once you look away, you will forget who they are. It's fitting that these enemies attack the memory. In effect, they are the enemies of Time itself. You cannot remember the Silence, therefore they have no past. The Silence call themselves the "sentinels of history," which is ironic considering their chief skill is erasing it.

Eventually, the Doctor comes to realize that he and River Song must physically touch in order to restart time. "We're the opposite poles of the disruption," the Doctor says. "If we touch, we short out the differential. Time can begin again." By touching, River and the Doctor are in the same time and place once again, which straightens out the temporal confusion. It's Whovian logic, but it works. We leap back to Lake Silencio, where the Doctor dies just as he always did, and across the universe, Time begins to chuff along at its normal pace. But the Doctor has one final trick, as he always does. Before long, he appears, resurrected and in fine fettle, ready to dash off on more adventures and cheat death yet again.

In the book of Ecclesiastes, Solomon describes the inexorability of Time as a burden wearing down the sons of men:

> What has been is what will be,
> and what has been done is what will be done,
> and there is nothing new under the sun.
> Is there a thing of which it is said,
> "See, this is new"?
> It has been alrady in the ages before us.
> There is no remembrance of former things,
> nor will there be any remembrance of later things yet to be
> among those who come after. (Eccl. 1:9–11)

Solomon is not overly impressed with the way the world rolls on and on and goes nowhere. In fact, he's sick of it. It appears that Man is doomed to work all his days and see no lasting fruit for his efforts. Timelessness sounds like a blessing.

Solomon is speaking from a man's point of view. From God's point of view, this repetition is anything but a chore.[13] G. K. Chesterton puts it wonderfully:

> Grown-up people are not strong enough to exult in monotony. But perhaps God is strong enough to exult in monotony. It is possible that God says every morning, "Do it again" to the sun; and every evening, "Do it again" to the moon. It may not be automatic necessity that makes all daisies alike; it may be that God makes every daisy separately, but has never got tired of making them. It may be that He has the eternal appetite of infancy; for we have sinned and grown old, and our Father is younger than we.[14]

We may think that repetition is equal to monotony, but that's because we bear the burdens of a sinful world. For our Father in heaven, Time abounds with infinite possibilities. Don't we know His mercies are new every morning?

God is not the one without a history. God is the one who remembers the covenants He made with His people.[15] Like the Doctor, He is the enemy of the Silence and champion of Time. What answer does He provide to Solomon's complaint? At the end of Ecclesiastes, Solomon concludes with this: "For God will bring every deed into judgment, with every secret thing, whether good or evil." (Eccl 12:14) Solomon tells us that the reason we can have hope alongside the pain of this life, the reason we can set a table in the mists, is that God is faithful, and He will bring every work into judgment. Without this assurance, we have nothing to live for. But knowing that God is in control of the shape of Time and that one day He will sort everything out, we can live in this repetitive, frustrating world and have hope for the future.

Solomon ends Ecclesiastes with hope, because he understands that God will "bring every deed into judgment." We also have that hope, which we call faith. And what gives strength to our faith? How can we be sure that Time will maintain the shape and structure God has given it? How do we know that we aren't trapped in a temporal tide pool, like Winston Churchill, the Holy Roman Emperor?

The death of the Doctor provides a fixed point in his universe, which gives shape to everything else. Unless his death occurs in the correct time and the correct place, Time ceases to move with any kind of sense or direction. "This is a fixed point," the Doctor says to River, who is about to kill him. "This must happen. This always happens." And when it does happen as it should, the universe is saved.

In our world, Christ's death performs a similar role. We believe that Christ's death changed the future, which is correct, but we should be careful not to be too narrow in our thinking. The shockwaves from Christ's death reached both backwards and forwards across Time.[16] This "fixed point in Time" affects everything in our lives, past and future. It gives the Christian a history, a present community, and a future hope.

Watching *Doctor Who* gives the viewer the feeling that the order in which things happen is unimportant as long as everything gets done eventually. The Doctor and his companions time-travel regularly to ensure that causes and effects happen where they should, so that one thing will lead to another. All of these timey-wimey shenanigans seem to be the stuff of science fiction, but there is a sense it which we experience the same thing, every single week during church worship.

Liturgy is one of the places in everyday life where time and eternity come together. When worshipers participate in a liturgy, such as the Lord's Supper, they are participating in the history of the Church. "Do this in remembrance of me," Jesus said.[17] By doing this, we proclaim the Lord's death (past event) until He comes (future event). The entire story of the Church: past, present, and future, is summarized in this ritual.

Christians are a people of Time. They are loci of the past and the future. Because God is not bound to a specific time, there is no such thing as "too late." He can and will bring all things to judgment in His own good time. We on earth are simply called to wait, living faithfully until God fulfills the promise He made in Isaiah:

Before they call, I will answer;
while they are yet speaking, I will hear. (Isaiah 65:24)

ENDNOTES

1   Samuel Alexander, *The Collected Works of Samuel Alexander* (New York: Continuum International Publishing Group, 2000), 349. Quoted in Staffan Bergsten, *Time and Eternity: A Study in the Structure and Symbolism of the Works of T.S. Eliot* (Stockholm: Svenska Bokförlaget, 1960), 28.

2   Boethius, *The Consolation of Philosophy*, ed. James T. Buchanan (New York: Frederick Ungar, 1957).

3   C. S. Lewis, *Mere Christianity* (San Francisco, CA: HarperSanFrancisco, 2009).

4   William Lane Craig, *Time and Eternity: Exploring God's Relationship to Time* (Wheaton, IL: Crossway, 2001), 14.

5   Lewis, *Mere Christianity*.

6   T.S. Eliot, *Four Quartets* (New York: Mariner Books, 1968).

7   Except for perhaps in "The Curse of Fatal Death." In that episode The Doctor invites the Master to meet him in a ruined castle on the planet Tersurus "in two hour's relative time." When the Doctor arrives he finds the Master gloating, because he has travelled a century back in time and bribed the castle's architect to install a secret death trap. But the Doctor had known this would happen and had travelled further back, bribed the same architect to sabotage the trap. The Master foresaw that, and arranged for an additional trap leading to the vast sewers of Tersurus . . . and the gag continues on and on. This spoof episode for Red Nose Day features Rowan Atkinson (Ninth Doctor), Richard E. Grant (Tenth Doctor), Jim Broadbent (Eleventh Doctor), Hugh Grant (Twelfth Doctor), Joanna Lumley (Thirteenth Doctor), Jonathan Pryce (The Master), and Julia Sawalha (Emma, the Doctor's Companion).

8   "Silence in the Library."

9   "The Impossible Astronaut."

10   "The Life and Death of River Song."

11   "Blink."

12   G. K. Chesterton, *Orthodoxy* (San Francisco: Ignatius Press, reprint 1995).

13   See Psalm 104.

14   Chesterton, *Orthodoxy*.

15   See Ps 105:8.

16   See Hebrews 9.

17   See Luke 22:19.

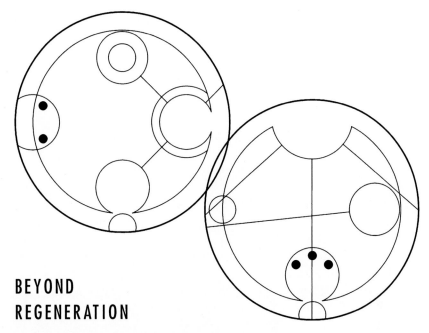

BEYOND
REGENERATION

TRANSFORMATION: *Empty Child/The Doctor Dances*
ORIGINAL AIRDATE: MAY 21/28 2005

There are many mind boggling things about *Doctor Who*—a police box that is bigger on the inside, multiple regenerations of the same person working together in the same episode, the bending of history so much so that it can make bow ties cool. Then there is the thing that boggles my mind the most: *how much an atheist has to teach me about God.*

I am thinking of Russell T Davies, the mad scientist that rebooted the series with the Ninth Doctor (played by Christopher Eccleston). Davies would be at the helm of the TARDIS, beginning with Eccleston and continuing through the David Tennant years. I am continually amazed by the way in which key aspects of my faith are played out in the action of those episodes. Grace, faith, forgiveness, justice, and mercy all appear in *Doctor Who.*

I want to be clear here—I am in no way claiming that Davies set out to make a defense for the Church. In fact, Russell[1] is an avowed atheist.[2] I imagine that last role he would consider is Defender of the Faith or that of an apologist, helping to illustrate the nuances of Christianity.

But he is a writer, one with talent and a willingness to let the work speak. And he works in the Sci-Fi world, a sphere known for exploring big themes.

Among the big themes of humanity are those often left to the theologians and philosophers.

When asked if he intentionally seeks to explore social, political or religious themes in his writing, Davies said,

> It's tricky, that social/political/religious thing, because really that's *life*, that's *people*, that's *what you think about the world,* and that's why you want to write in the first place. It's not like there's a section of my mind that categorizes things—like, this scene is about character, the next is all sociology. They're all in there, in one huge continuum.[3]

So I see God at every turn in the Doctor's adventures. One aspect of God's work in His Creation is that of redemptive transformation. When talking transformation and the Doctor, the mind jumps immediately to regeneration; however, I want to look at how not the Doctor but instead the show's *other* characters are transformed.

Let's start by digging into a two-part episode from Series One, featuring the Ninth Doctor, his Companion Rose, and the first[4] appearance of Captain Jack Harkness.

"THE EMPTY CHILD" AND "THE DOCTOR DANCES"

In the frequently bombarded, WWII London, a ghostly boy of five, wearing a gas mask, wanders the streets calling for his mummy. The child doesn't seem to have much vocabulary beyond asking, "Are you my mummy?"

Oh, and he isn't *wearing* a gas mask, his face *is* a gas mask. And anyone he touches becomes sick, dies, and is reanimated with a face turned into a gas mask.

Creepy.

The boy targets a girl named Nancy, following her throughout the town, persistently asking, "Are you my mummy?"

The Doctor comes into the story, tracking the strangeness to a hospital full of gas-masked, reanimated patients. He narrowly escapes with his life. Eventually, the Doctor is able to determine the source of the trouble: a space ambulance that has crashed in London. The ambulance was full of microscopic, medical nanogenes—healing by invading the body of the patient and rebuilding the DNA to replace the sickly parts.

When the ambulance crashed, the only "patient" nearby was the boy— already dead and wearing a gas mask. The nanogenes didn't know what a human was supposed to be, and assuming the gas mask was a face, rebuilt the boy as best they could—animated outside, dead inside.

But the toxic micro-doctors were not finished. They then assumed that all of humanity was supposed to be like this dead boy—and so whenever the nano-genes are transferred to another, they remake the new person in the image of the scared, masked boy looking for his mother.

At the climax of the story, the Doctor, Nancy, Rose and Jack are at the site of the crash, and the Doctor has figured out what the nanogenes are doing. But, alas, there is no weapon that can stop the little healers from destroying all of humanity.

All the gas-maskers arrive led by the little boy, still calling for his mummy.

And the Doctor figures out one more thing—why the boy keeps chasing Nancy. Up to now, it has been believed (based on Nancy's own testimony) that the boy is her brother. But she is a bit older than she looks.

The Doctor encourages her to face the truth, and answer the child.

THE DOCTOR: He's gonna keep asking, Nancy. He's never gonna stop. Tell him.
No answer. The gas mask people begin to walk forward.
THE DOCTOR: Nancy... the future of the human race is in your hands. Trust me... and tell him.
Nancy sniffs, still tearful. The Child approaches them.
THE CHILD: Are you my mummy?
The Doctor gives Nancy a gentle push in the direction of the Child.
THE CHILD: Are you my mummy? Are you my mummy?
NANCY: (*whispers*) Yes. (*stronger*) Yes. I AM your mummy.
She faces him. The Child walks slowly forward.
THE CHILD: Mummy?
NANCY: I'm here.
THE CHILD: Are you my mummy?
NANCY: (*kneeling before him*) I'm here.
THE CHILD: Are you my mummy?
NANCY: (*whispers*) Yes.
THE DOCTOR: (*to Rose*) He doesn't understand. There's not enough of him left.
Nancy looks at her little boy.
NANCY: (*tearful, sincere*) I am your mummy. I will always be your mummy. I'm so sorry.
And she takes him into her arms, no longer caring what will happen to her-self. The nanogenes surround them, making them glow with a golden light.[5]

Please note that little bit of action—*she takes him into her arms, no longer caring what will happen to herself.*

The nanogenes envelop the duo in their sparkly light, entering Nancy and the child. When they separate, the boy takes off his gas mask—back from the dead and fully healed.

The Doctor explains to Rose, Jack, and the viewers what has happened. The nanogenes recognized the mother as the true model, and corrected their mistake. Then, with prompting from the Doctor, the nanogenes revisit all the people they've corrupted, and heal them.

And not just from the damage done by the nanogenes—but from all prior damage. All of the formerly gas-masked patients are now in perfect health.

Transformed.

Redeemed.

Here are a few things that I took away from these stories.

TRANSFORMATION STARTS WITH AN ACT OF LOVE

The Child is hurting. Not just physically, but spiritually. He is dead inside, lost, not knowing who he is or to whom he belongs.

But his mother knows who he is. Her words are not enough; the Child can't understand "just words."

So she reaches out, touches him. She takes him in her arms. Such behavior is reminiscent of the actions of another caregiver, Mother Teresa.[6]

> When she took in her hands the paper-thin hands of men or women she communicated with them by the consoling stroke of her strong fingers.[7]

Both the fictional Nancy and non-fictional Mother Teresa were following another model. One from history. Here is one of His stories:

> Jesus of Nazareth was traveling about with his disciples, teaching and healing. One day as they walked along a road, they came across a leper.
>
> Leprosy is a highly contagious disease that disfigures the victim; in that day there was no known cure. As such, lepers where labeled "unclean," and laws strictly forbade any physical contact.
>
> This leper fell in the path of Jesus and the disciples.
>
> "Lord, if you are willing, you can make me clean," he called out.
>
> So what did Jesus do? Not caring what would happen to Himself, He reached out and touched the leper, saying,
>
> "I am willing. Be clean."
>
> And the man was instantly cured of his disease. He went about the countryside, blabbing about his healing, which brought even more crowds to the Healer.[8]

Note that Jesus reached out and touched the leper. He didn't have to do that. We know from Jesus' healing of the Centurion's servant that Jesus could have said the word, and the healing force would have traversed the gulf.[9]

But he touched the guy. What's up with that?

I think Jesus was not simply healing the leper's body. Sure the guy was a leper, and that's bad. But he was also hurting in the soul—he was an untouchable, a persona non grata. What's that term we use these days for someone who is a social outcast, who should be avoided at all costs? Yeah, that's right—a leper.

Jesus reached out and touched the untouchable, held the unclean, showed love to the unloved. Sure he could have just spoken the words, and the man's body would be healed. But, like the gas-masked child, the man's soul might not have understood the words.

It took an act of love to make him completely whole.

Pope John Paul II explains it this way:

> Love, above all, possesses a saving power. The saving power of love, according to the words of Saint Paul in the First Letter to the Corinthians, is greater than that of mere knowledge of the truth: "So faith, hope, love remain, these three; but the greatest of these is love," (1 Cor 13:13) Salvation through love is, at the same time, a sharing in the fullness of truth, and also in the fullness of beauty. All this is God.[10]

TRANSFORMATION IS RISKY

When Nancy knelt down and reached for her child, she was risking her very life. It wasn't even a risk; a risk implies a possibility of survival. Nancy was *guaranteeing* her own death with her act of love. But that didn't matter; at this point all that mattered was that her child was lost, and needed his mummy.

When Jesus reached out to the leper, he was making the same risk, that of taking on the disease of the lost one.

Reaching out with an act of love is risky business. Journalist and activist Eileen Egan recognized this risk in her own actions, as they did not match up to Mother Teresa's.

> As I followed Mother Teresa, a few waving hands were held out to me, expecting that I, too, would stop, for a consoling touch. I knew that along with starvation most of the diseases known to humankind were in that enclosure. I was shortly to leave for Vietnam. Trembling and ashamed, I turned away.[11]

There is a very moving, deeply powerful moment in "The Doctor Dances." Thing is, I completely missed it first go around, because I didn't have a clue as to how ridiculously earth-shattering that moment was. It is after the nanogenes start to learn, and the Doctor makes a plea to the universe:

THE DOCTOR: Oh, come on. Give me a day like this. Give me this one.

He is indeed given "this one," and the nanogenes do their work. And not only is the boy healed, but everyone is healed.

THE DOCTOR: (*ecstatic*) Everybody lives, Rose. Just this once. Everybody lives!

That's the moment. The deep, deep moment: the joy of the Doctor is un-bounded, he has reason to dance—everybody lives! After watching the following few years with David Tennant, I began to understand why it was so signifi-cant . . . because it was so rare.

Yes, the Doctor saves the day, time after time. But it always comes at a cost. In the end, the majority of humanity is all right; but along the way, many are lost. This is one source of the Doctor's deep sadness—the weight of those that weren't saved in the process of saving those that are.

Doing right has a price; conquering evil has a cost. The following is a letter underscoring this truth. It is a real letter, written by an American OSS officer to his son. One of the many remarkable things about this war relic is that it was written on Adolf Hitler's stationary. The letter says:

Dear Dennis,

The man who might have written on this card once controlled Europe—three short years ago when you were born. Today he is dead, his memory de-spised, his country in ruins. He had a thirst for power, a low opinion of man as an individual, and a fear of intellectual honesty. He was a force for evil in the world. His passing, his defeat—a boon to mankind. But thousands died that it might be so. The price for ridding society of bad is always high.

Love, Daddy[12]

The Doctor has a right to dance—he has been given a great gift. For once, once! Everybody lives!

For the wages of sin is death, but the gift of God is eternal life.

TRANSFORMATION IS A GIFT FROM THE OUTSIDE

The Doctor is the hero of *Doctor Who*, and writing rules are very clear that the story must be about the hero. The hero must be the one who has the goal, who is blocked by the obstacle, who drives the plot, and most of all, who saves the day.

So it seems that "The Empty Child" and "The Doctor Dances" breaks the cardinal rules. Oh, the Doctor clearly has the quest, faces the antagonist and drives the plot. But the Doctor is not the one who saves the day.

No, Nancy takes the first step in saving the day, in her dangerous act of love. But even Nancy is not the one that heals the empty child, nor restores the other gas mask victims. It is the nanogenes, that outside force, that heals.

This works on a dramatic level in part because it speaks to a deeper truth: the Doctor can do many near miraculous things, and while he can race *against* time and death, he cannot defeat them. No one can.

Pope John Paul II points this truism this way:

> The world is not able to free man from suffering; specifically it is not able to free him from death.[13]

TRANSFORMATION AND GRACE

The idea of grace from outside is the major theme of the episode "Boomtown," by Russell T. Davies. Here's the story:

The Doctor catches Margaret (aka Blon Fel Fotch), a Slitheen[14] who has twice now tried to destroy the earth. First go around it was to sell off bits of radioactive earth for profit; this time to power a vessel[15] to get home.

The Doctor decides to take her home—and turn her over to the authorities. But here's the twist: Margaret's home world has the death penalty, and Margaret has already been tried and sentenced in absentia. Going home means being punished by death.

Before they can go, the TARDIS needs to be powered up, so they have some time to kill.

I should mention a thing or two about the TARDIS.[16] It is powered by something called "the Heart of the TARDIS"—a sentient energy within the big blue box.

The Heart of the TARDIS is an ephemeral force, a spirit form. She is telepathic, and can guide the Doctor even from a distance. The Doctor travels where he likes, but the Heart will often nudge him (or push him) to specific times and locales.

And the Heart has the gift of tongues—she is the universal translator for all who travel within her ship. All characteristics that could be applied to the Christian understanding of the Holy Spirit—all the way down to the giver of the gift of tongues.

Margaret is very impressed by the TARDIS.

MARGARET: I almost feel better about being defeated. We never stood a chance. This is the technology of the gods.
THE DOCTOR: Don't worship me—I'd make a very bad god. You wouldn't get a day off, for starters.

Anywho, the Doctor and company are waiting for the Heart to get refueled, and that leaves some time for Margaret to plead her case with the Doctor. And she has all kinds of reasons why she feels the Doctor should let her avoid the death penalty.

First she tries a little guilt: if the Doctor takes her in, that makes him a murderer, right? The argument is ignored—another's transgression doesn't make Margaret any less guilty.

Then she tries to get the Doctor to pity her—and he does. But having pity on someone doesn't erase his or her guilt, nor his or her debt.

Then she argues that she has changed, that she won't be trying to destroy the world again. The Doctor counters this, saying that change isn't in her nature. After all, she twice tries to poison the time lord while making these pleas.

Then she provides proof that she can be virtuous. There was a woman that she was going to kill, but she didn't. See, she did a good thing!

THE DOCTOR: It doesn't mean anything.
MARGARET: I spared her life.
THE DOCTOR: You let one of them go, but that's nothing new. Every now and then, a little victim's spared. Because she smiled . . . because he's got freckles . . . 'cos they begged . . . and that's how you live with yourself. That's how you slaughter millions. Because once in a while, on a whim, if the wind's in the right direction . . . you happen to be kind.

In other words, doing some good doesn't erase the bad that you did.

Her last attempt for clemency is to argue that she is not responsible for her own behavior. It is just the way she was raised; it was her community, her environment, not her.

Yeah, the Doctor doesn't buy that either.

There is nothing that Margaret can do or say to be saved.

So Margaret forgoes arguing, turns the tables on the Doctor, and prepares to use the TARDIS to blow up the world and ride her surfboard to freedom.

But in doing so, she exposes herself to the Heart of the TARDIS. Bathed in its light, really.

Breathing heavily, Margaret stares into the light, as if forgetting everything else. Her voice becomes dreamy and vague.

MARGARET: It's... so bright...
THE DOCTOR: Look at it, Margaret...
MARGARET: ... Beautiful...
THE DOCTOR: Look inside, Blon Fel Fotch. Look at the light.
    Margaret is transfixed by the light, and her grip on Rose relaxes. Rose stumbles out of the way and back to Jack. Margaret continues to stare into the light, a blissful smile spreading across her face. Then, she looks up at the Doctor who smiles slightly.
MARGARET: (*softly, genuinely*) Thank you...
    She is engulfed by the light, and when it clears, her body-suit flops on top of the extrapolator, empty.

She's not dead, as one (or at least Jack) might suppose. Rather, the Spirit that has engulfed her transforms her back into an egg.

ROSE: She's an egg?
THE DOCTOR: Regressed to her childhood.
JACK: She's an egg?
THE DOCTOR: She can start again! Live her life from scratch. If we take her home, give her to a different family, tell 'em to bring her up properly, she might be all right!
JACK: Or she might be worse.
THE DOCTOR: That's her choice.
ROSE: She's an egg.
THE DOCTOR: She's an egg.

And thus, has a chance to be saved.
    It's not pity, or good deeds, or promises or threats—the only way to be avoid the death penalty, the only true grace, is to be bathed by the Spirit and born again. "Immortality is not a part of this world. It can only come to man exclusively from God."[17] Or as Jesus once told Nicodemus, "Very truly I tell you, no one can see the kingdom of God unless they are born again."[18]

TRANSFORMATION IS CONTAGIOUS

The gas mask disease is proven to be contagious; anyone the boy touches dies. Anyone that a victim of the boy touches dies. The disease is exponential in its spread.

That is why the Doctor stays away from the touch of the inflicted; that is why Nancy hesitates to come to her child's rescue; that is why the leper is labeled unclean, and forced to stand off at a distance.

But then child is redeemed, transformed, healed. And just as the spread of the disease is contagious, so is the redemption. All who are sick catch the cure, and are made whole. The chain is broken, and starts a chain-reaction. Philip Yancy writes,

> The gospel of grace begins and ends with forgiveness. And people write songs with titles like "Amazing Grace" for one reason: grace is the only force in the universe powerful enough to break the chains that enslave generations. Grace alone melts ungrace.[19]

Jesus, too, understood the nature of contagion. He warned against the yeast of false teaching, how it would spread and destroy the whole of the loaf of bread.[20]

And he told of the cure, how the yeast of the kingdom can also spread like a virus.[21] Jesus also spoke of the kingdom as a mustard seed—starting out small, but soon growing to be able to house nest upon nest of birds.[22]

This is the model of the church, isn't it? A sick person is made whole from the inside out. That person models the love of Christ that saved them—and that love gets passed on to another.

> God wants us to become contagious Christians—His agents who will first catch his love and then urgently and infectiously offer it to all who are willing to consider it. This is His primary plan, the one Jesus modeled so powerfully, to spread God's grace and truth person to person until there's an epidemic of changed lives around the world.[23]

TRANSFORMATION MODELS HEALTHY DNA

In "The Doctor Dances," the nanogenes do not change their process. When everyone is saved—when "everyone lives"—it isn't because the nanogenes change their method and start doing something different. What has changed isn't the nanogenes; rather it is their source. They were working off of a dead DNA sample; but when Nancy steps forward in love, they find the real thing.

The truth is, we are all transforming—every single last one of us. We are either in process of changing into dead inside, lost, mummy-calling gas maskers, or we are transforming into something else. It all depends on what DNA source we are mining. The key is to find healthy DNA to model. And if we want complete redemptive transformation, we need to find a perfect sample.

Mother Teresa's work used a two-step process. The first was to recognize the perfect sample in those they reached out to, the sick and lost, and see them for the redeemed beings they could be.

> "Our work," Mother Teresa explained, "Calls for us to see Jesus in everyone. Jesus has told us that he is the hungry one, the naked one, the thirsty one. He is the one without a home. He is the one who is suffering ... They are Jesus. Each one is Jesus in a distressing disguise."[24]

Then once Jesus was identified in the ailing person, it then became the job of the caregiver to become Jesus for that person.

> ... So that one can see Christ in every human being. To transmit that vision to others so that the result is a complete transformation of life is a mystery beyond telling, a mystery of grace.[25]

Jesus indeed is the perfect DNA sample, the one we are to model.[26] St. Paul tells us that if we are in Christ, we are a new creation,[27] modeled on Christ. It is from that perfect DNA sample that we can become like Him—compassionate, kind, humble, gentle, and patient.[28]

Interestingly enough, being transformed into little Christs has one other consequence: we are to be the transformation agent in others. We are to model his redemptive love by loving redemptively, just as Nancy and Teresa loved.

We are to love dangerously and infectiously. "To save means to embrace and lift up with redemptive love, with love that is always greater than any sin."[29]

And if we model our new DNA correctly, the Doctor teaches us that we will have just one more job to do.

Dance.

ENDNOTES

1   I feel that I may call him Russell as we spent an afternoon together—I was about fifty-three rows back from the stage when he appeared at ComicCon.

2   In his own words: "And I'm not even superstitious. I was born atheist, me." Benjamin Cook and Russell T. Davies. *Dr. Who, The Writer's Tale: The Untold Story of the BBC Series* (London: BBC Books, 2008), 18.

3   *The Writer's Tale*, 35. Davies followed up with this thought: "I say the process is inevitable, but also I do think it's your job as a writer to say something about the world. Why else are you writing?"

4   Or did Jack first appear in the second episode of Series One, "The End of the World"?

5   Quoting from the show was made easier by the fine transcribing work of *Doctor Who* 2005+ Transcripts (http://who-transcripts.atspace.com/). Throughout this chapter, all quotes are taken from these transcripts.

6   The Doctor and Mother Teresa share many traits, and not just as people who travel where they are not asked to help those that can't help themselves. In describing how she chooses her missions, Mother Teresa said: "In the choice of works, there was neither planning nor per-conceived ideas. We started the work as the suffering of the people called us. God showed us what to do." Neither planning nor preconceived ideas—sure sounds like the Doctor to me. Egan, Eileen M. "Blessed are the Merciful: Mother Teresa (1910–1997)." America 177, 7 (September 20, 1997). 13.

7   Egan, 9.

8   My broad paraphrase of Matthew 8:1-4.

9   Matthew 8:5-13.

10   John Paul II. *Crossing the Threshold of Hope.* New York: Knopf, 2005. 74.

11   Egan, 9.

12   www.lettersofnote.com A wonderful site reprinting significant letters and notes from history.

13   John Paul II, *Crossing the Threshold of Hope,* 56.

14   The Slitheen are a family of Raxacoricofallapatorian criminals. Alien race, don't 'cha know. Of all the aliens created following the Doctor's ninth regeneration, the Slitheen have been featured the most, having appeared in six television stories, two books and one short story.

15   A cosmic surf board, really. Not to be confused with the Silver Surfer's cosmic surf board, which is powered by a tiny portion of Galactus's Power Cosmic.

16   TARDIS stands for "Time And Relative Dimension In Space" and it is the space/time ship in which the Doctor travels. According to "Journey's End" a TARDIS is meant to have six pilots. During operation, the TARDIS has a distinctive grinding *vworp-vworp* sound, although River Song once demonstrated that it is capable of materializing silently. The core element of TARDIS technology is the space-time element, or the Heart. During the times of the Fifth, Ninth, Tenth, and Eleventh Doctors, it was located beneath the central console.

17   John Paul II, *Crossing the Threshold of Hope,* 56.

18   John 3:3.

19   Philip Yancey. *What's So Amazing About Grace?* (Grand Rapids, MI: Zondervan Publishing House, 1997), 90.

20   Matthew 13:33

21   Matthew 16:6.

22   Matthew 13:31–32.

23   Bill Hybels and Mark Mittleberg, *Becoming a Contagious Christian.* (Grand Rapids, MI: Zondervan,   1994), 23.

24   Egan, 9.

25   Egan, 18.

26   John 13:13, I Corinthians 11:1, Ephesians 5:1–2, Colossians 3:13, 1 Peter 2:20–22, 1 John 2:6; to name but a few.

27   2 Corinthians 5:17.

28   Colossians 3:10-12.

29   John Paul II, *Crossing the Threshold of Hope,* 58.

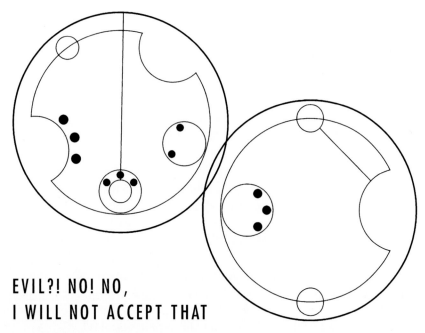

EVIL?! NO! NO,
I WILL NOT ACCEPT THAT

EVIL: *Genesis of the Daleks*
ORIGINAL AIRDATE: MARCH 8, 1975

Throughout history, humanity has asked a profound question: how do we reconcile the existence of evil with the existence of God? Some have chosen to say that evil, as we understand it, doesn't really exist. In his much-publicized *Nightline* debate with Pastor Mark Driscoll, Deepak Chopra boldly asserted that evil doesn't really exist; there are just some people who are more primitive than others.[1] Others have chosen to redefine the notion of God in such a way that He no longer looks like the God we find revealed to us in the Biblical scriptures. The only way God could exist in a world where evil exists, they assert, would be for God to either be unloving, or limited in His power[2].

The German philosopher, Gottfried Leibniz, coined the term "theodicy" to describe the pursuit of reconciling evil with the existence of God in his 1710 work, *Theodicy: Essays on the Goodness of God, the Freedom of Man and the Origin of Evil*. More recently, Notre Dame philosopher and apologist Alvin Plantinga has defined theodicy as "the answer to the question of why God permits evil."[3] *The Blackwell Companion to Philosophy* takes the purpose of theodicy a step further, stating, "A theodicy seeks to show that it is reasonable to believe in God despite evidence of evil in the world and offers a framework which can account for why evil exists."[4]

However one chooses to define or frame an explanation for how evil and God could co-exist, the question remains a lingering concern for many, regardless of their spiritual beliefs or backgrounds. I remember getting ready to study the concept in seminary, and feeling overjoyed that finally, after years of spiritual inquiry, this profound question of mine would be answered. Like a broken TARDIS, however, the answer never materialized; at least not in the manner I had hoped. As I interacted with some of the greatest Christian thinkers throughout history, I realized that whenever we interact with a theodicy, if we hope to remain orthodox in our understanding of God, there are some things we can say, and other things we cannot. Ultimate answers don't always come to us in the manner we would like. We need to be comfortable living in a certain amount of tension, knowing that while some answers have been revealed to us, according to Deuteronomy 29:29, there will always exist certain "secret things" that belong to God alone.

Philosophers and theologians do not own a corner on the market when it comes to addressing issues surrounding the existence of evil. Science fiction has been dealing with this, and other profound metaphysical topics, for years, especially in the annals of history as communicated in *Doctor Who*.

Doctor Who, perhaps more-so than any other science fiction franchise, perfectly allows for this kind of reflection. In many ways, the Doctor can be seen as a "god-like" character, in that he and God share some attributes that humanity and God do not. For example, Systematic Theologian Louis Berkhof speaks of God being both immense and omnipresent. He is immense in that He "transcends all space and is not subject to its limitations..." and He is omnipresent in that He "fills every part of space with His entire Being..."[5] Similarly, The Doctor, as a Time Lord, has the ability to transcend space and its limitations (he can even be two places at the same time, as we see in episodes that simultaneously bring several Doctors together).[6] However, he can also materialize almost anywhere and anytime, granting him certain omnipresent characteristics.

Theologian A.W. Pink speaks of God's omniscience, which he describes as God's ability to "know everything; everything possible, everything actual; all events and all creatures, of the past, present, and future."[7] The Doctor, while not exhaustively possessing this attribute, does have potentially unlimited access to knowledge of events and people; past, present, and future. In literary terms, he would have an "omniscient point of view" when it comes to certain events[8].

God's omnipresence and omniscience rarely get mentioned without also including God's omnipotence. In Job 42:2, Job says of God "I know that You can do all things; no plan of yours can be thwarted." J.I. Packer uses this scripture to describe God's omnipotence, saying, "Omnipotence means in practice the power to do everything that in His power and moral perfection (i.e. his wisdom and goodness) God wills to do."[9] Likewise, The Doctor, though limited in his power, can still potentially exercise near omnipotent power, by combining his other near-divine attributes and using them to manipulate key historical events. If part of God's omnipotence includes His sovereign control over historical events, the Doctor, should he choose, could also operate in a similar manner.

This brings us to the present topic: *Doctor Who* and the Problem of Evil. As the study of theodicy has shown us, we could spend eons discussing the various aspects of this problem. Since we do not have access to a TARDIS and the ability to create a temporal vortex wherein the effects of time could be temporarily suspended, I will limit the purview of this discussion to two related topics. First, we will examine a common apologetics question, and second we will examine the redemption of evil.

As a missions minded, church planting Anglican priest, I spent much of my time in conversations with people at local coffee-shops. I listen to their stories, and often ask pointed questions concerning what they believe about spiritual matters; then I listen. Many people, both inside and outside the church, have difficultly reconciling the idea that a benevolent God, characterized by all the attributes we just mentioned, could exist in light of all the evil they see in the world. The question makes sense. After all, if an all-powerful God has the ability to stop evil, but doesn't, doesn't that make Him evil?

Doctor Who has addressed this question, and its implications, in one form or another plenty of times over the past fifty years. For example, the 2011 episode "Let's Kill Hitler" opens by introducing us to Mels, the lifelong best friend of Amy Pond, the Doctor's Companion. Growing up, Amy had often told Mels stories about the Time traveling Doctor who had once saved her life and promised to return. In this episode, Mels finally meets the Doctor, and says something that many would say, if we suddenly realized we had the ability to travel through time.

"You've got a time machine, I've got a gun. What the hell. Let's kill Hitler."

The episode then shows a flashback of Amy and Mels as teenagers in a history class. Mels responds to a teacher's question by answering, "A significant factor in Hitler's rise to power was the fact that the Doctor didn't stop him."[10]

This kind of reaction is understandable. If we had the means, the knowledge, and the ability to somehow prevent the reign of one of the most wicked people in modern history, wouldn't we have a moral obligation to do so? If we could travel back in time and kill Hitler, the lives of six million Jews could be saved.

That particular episode did not end up directly addressing this question, but it was dealt with more directly in "Genesis of the Daleks,"[11] the third episode during Tom Baker's run as the Fourth Doctor. The Daleks (the Doctor's most iconic enemy) were created by Terry Nation, who grew up during World War II, and had vivid memories of the fear caused by German bombings. He decided to base the Daleks on the Nazis, and portrayed them as cruel, heartless creatures, bent on total conquest and the elimination of any race that didn't meet their standards[12].

In *The Genesis of the Daleks*, the Doctor, along with his companions Sara Jane Smith and Harry Sullivan, find themselves transported to the planet Skaro, the home-world of the Daleks. The Time Lords have sent the Doctor there on a mission to interfere with the Dalek's creation, in order to prevent them from conquering the universe in the future. The episode introduces Davros, the wicked scientist who mutates his own race in order to create the Daleks as a super-warrior race, free from the limitations caused by all emotions except for hate.

In a pivotal scene, the Doctor has an opportunity to destroy the entire brood of gestating Daleks before they are hatched. All he has to do is connect two wires, and an explosive device will detonate in the room harboring the Daleks, destroying them all before their reign of terror even begins. However, the Doctor pauses.

A confused Sara presses him. "What are you waiting for?" she asks.

"Just touch these two strands together and the Daleks are finished," the Doctor responds, but then he interjects a question that shows the reason for his pause. "Have I that right?"

We can imagine the thoughts going through the Doctor's mind. He has the means, the knowledge, and the ability, to prevent the creation of one of the most wicked races in the universe's history; does he or doesn't he have a moral obligation to do so? Sara responds in the affirmative.

"To destroy the Daleks? You can't doubt it."

The Doctor's response, however, echoes responses given by two "Doctors of the Church,"[13] St. Augustine, and Thomas Aquinas.

"Well, I do. You see, some things could be better with the Daleks. Many future worlds will become allies just because of their fear of the Daleks."

St. Augustine, the brilliant fourth century theologian, laid the groundwork for most of the future discussions concerning the goodness of God and the existence of evil in his *Enchiridion*. He writes,

> In this universe, even what is called evil, when it is rightly ordered and kept in its place, commends the good more eminently, since good things yield greater pleasure and praise when compared to the bad things. For the Omnipotent God... would not allow any evil in his works, unless in his omnipotence and goodness, as the Supreme Good, he is able to bring forth good out of evil.[14]

For Augustine, evil like we see in the Daleks could serve two benevolent purposes. First, by way of comparison, it could help us see the beauty and goodness of the universe with more clarity. One can better appreciate the goodness of a peaceful Gallifreyan sunset, after exposure to the horrors wrought by the Daleks' intergalactic destructive rampages. Sometimes, the horror of war makes it possible for people to appreciate life's simple beauties.

Second, God, being supremely good, could bring good out of evil. This thinking had a profound impact on Thomas Aquinas, the great thirteenth century theologian and philosopher, who attempted to synthesize Aristotelian Philosophy with a Biblically based worldview. His writings, perhaps more-so than anyone else's, shaped what would become modern day philosophical thought. His most profound collection of writings, *The Summa Theologica*, addresses such issues as the nature of God, man, morality, and included proofs for God's existence.

Drawing heavily from Augustine, Aquinas also attempted to reconcile God's goodness with the existence of evil. "This is part of the infinite goodness of God," he wrote, "that he should allow evil to exist, and out of it produce good."[15] Applying this principle to the *Genesis of the Daleks*, we can see the reason for the Doctor's hesitance. The Daleks' existence, though it caused great evil, also caused various societies across the universe to become allies in order to fight them off. If the Doctor destroyed the Daleks at this juncture, the "good" that would have come about because of these alliances would never happen. Therefore, at least according to Augustine and Aquinas, the Doctor's decision to allow the Daleks to come into existence would not be an evil decision, nor would it be a decision that would make the Doctor inherently evil.

If, however, the Doctor obeyed the Time Lord's directive, and destroyed the Daleks prior to their creation, his goodness would be in question. When Sara Jane objects to his hesitance in destroying the Daleks, the Doctor responds, "Have I that right?... I kill, wipe out a whole intelligent life-form, then I become like them. I'd be no better than the Daleks."

Dietrich Bonhoeffer, a German pastor killed after a failed plot to execute Hitler, wrestled extensively with this idea. In his work *Ethics*, he wrote that "What is worse than doing evil, is being evil."[16] From his perspective, one could perform an act perceived by others as evil, and you wouldn't become evil yourself, so long as you didn't perpetrate it in a morally evil manner. Therefore, in a time of war, assisting in the assassination of an evil dictator for the purpose of ending the war and saving millions of lives would not necessarily make you evil. However, you must, as Bonhoeffer himself did, approach such a decision with great humility and trepidation.

When we first meet the Christopher Eccleston incarnation of the Doctor, he has returned to earth shortly after fighting the Time Wars against the Daleks. As far as he knows, his previous regeneration—the War Doctor—ended the Time Wars by destroying all the Daleks, along with his fellow Time Lords. Until the conclusion of the 50th anniversary episode, *The Day of the Doctor*,[17] we see the Doctor wrestling with guilt over what he did to the Daleks. Was he any different than the Daleks when he exterminated all the Daleks?

We see this internal tension in the episode *Dalek*, where the Doctor confronts a lone Dalek, who thinks he now exists alone in the universe. The Dalek asks what he should do with himself, to which the Doctor gives this surprising response: "Why don't you kill yourself... rid the universe of your filth! Why don't you just die!!" The Dalek's response shocks the Doctor in to silence. "You would make a good Dalek."[18]

It would seem that any form of genocide, even against an evil enemy race, would be inherently evil, causing the perpetrator to become just as evil as the evil he tried to stop. In Bonhoeffer's case, genocide was not the issue, but the man committing mass genocide. Killing Hitler does not make someone evil; on the other hand, attempting to exterminate all Germans, just because they were German, would.

Ultimately, the Doctor chooses to take the higher ground, letting the nascent Daleks live. Sara Jane, who the writers often use to provide the voice of conscience for the Doctor, seems nonplussed by his decision. "If it was a disease or some sort of bacteria you were destroying, you wouldn't hesitate." The Doctor, however, seems convinced the Daleks must live. Sara Jane tries one more time to sway the Doctor with words that indirectly imply that if he lets the Daleks live, he will be culpable for all the evil they commit. "Think of all the suffering there'll be if you don't do it."

This final comment brings us back to the original question: if an all-powerful God has the ability to stop evil, but doesn't, does that make Him evil? In our context, the Doctor had the ability to stop a form of evil before it existed, yet he chooses not to. Does that make the Doctor evil? It would appear that, in actuality, killing the Daleks would make him evil. Letting them live shows his grace and mercy; attributes the Daleks do not possess. Further, it would appear that good can come about as a result of evil; therefore stopping the evil might prevent an even greater good from occurring. To prevent the greater good from ever happening would be a greater evil than the evil of the Daleks.

If that is the case, how then can we reconcile the existence of an all-powerful, benevolent God, with the existence of evil? The best place to look would be to the redemption of evil, a concept we find in Doctor Who, but also throughout Scripture.

We already looked at the creation of the Daleks, and how this evil led to a greater good, specifically the alliances that were formed because of their existence. This theme appears throughout the Doctor Who canon. For example, in *The Waters of Mars*[19], the Doctor accidentally visits the first Earth colony on Mars on the day that, he knows a mysterious nuclear explosion will destroy it. He then discovers the cause of the mysterious "fixed point in time" that eventually inspires humanity to push further and further into their exploration of space. The colony's captain, Adelaide Brooke, orders the outpost destroyed in order to prevent and evil Ice Warrior Virus from spreading to the Earth and taking over humanity. From the beginning, the viewers understand that greater good comes about as a result of this evil event.

Perhaps still dealing with guilt over what he did to the Daleks, the Doctor decides to break some of the laws of time and save Adelaide, however, when she realizes what he has done, she takes her own life so that the greater good can still occur. His attempts to assert himself as the "Time Lord Victorious" end tragically, and realizes that sometimes evil things must happen in order for the greater good to occur. Evil can ultimately serve a redemptive purpose.

We find this concept of evil serving a greater, redemptive purpose throughout Scripture. The first example is in the book of Job. In Job we see Satan, the personification of evil, appearing before the presence of God. He tells God that Job only lives righteously because he is so blessed by God. However, if Job were to experience evil in his life, he wouldn't be so quick to praise. God gives Satan permission to do as he pleases with Job, so long as he spares Job's life.[20] Job ends up losing almost everything, yet through it all he never curses God, nor does he ever realize the opening dialogue that occurred between God and Satan. The book ends with an incredible confession from Job 42:

> I know that you can do all things, and that no purpose of yours can be thwarted. 'Who is this that hides counsel without knowledge?' Therefore I have uttered what I did not understand, things too wonderful for me, which I did not know.

With these words, Job acknowledges that God can do anything; redeem evil in a way that Job can't yet fathom. The story concludes with Job receiving twice as many blessings from God as he had prior to Satan's attempted ruse.

The second example comes from the book of Genesis. The closing chapters tell us the story of Joseph, whose brothers do great evil toward him. They sell him off, and tell their father that he has died. Joseph ends up in slavery in Egypt. Many years pass, and this evil act allows Joseph to move up the ranks in Pharoah's kingdom. When a famine hits the region, Joseph's brothers have no choice but to go to Pharoah's kingdom and ask for food. Unbeknownst to them, they end up seeking help from Joseph, who grants it, and eventually reveals his identity to them. Horrified, they beg forgiveness, to which Joseph responds with these words, "As for you, you meant evil against me, but God meant it for good, to bring it about that many people should be kept alive, as they are today." (Genesis 50:20). Both Job and Joseph show us how God takes evil and uses it for a greater redemptive purpose.

The *Westminster Confession of Faith* explains that this is part of how God's providence works. He sovereignly governs all that comes to pass, yet manages to do so in such a manner as to not be culpable of sin. Sinfulness proceeds "only from the creature, and not from God, who, being most holy and righteous, neither is nor can be the author or approver of sin."[21] Theologian Karl Barth saw the evil that brought about human suffering as ultimately falling under the "control of divine providence."[22] There may be an element of mystery here, in terms of how that can work itself out, however, this theme runs throughout Scripture. We see the Apostle Paul applying this principle in Romans 8:28, when he says "And we know that for those who love God all things work together for good, for those who are called according to his purpose." In this context, "all things" would even include our sinful choices and actions. What we intend for evil, God uses for good.

We see evil most powerfully redeemed at the cross. During this horrific moment, all the principalities and powers of the universe conspired together to crucify Jesus. In John 13:2, we see Satan entering in to Judas Iscariot's heart before he turns Jesus over to be tried and crucified. In Acts 4: 27, believers in Jesus cry out to God, together, explaining what had happened at the crucifixion. ". . . for truly in this city there were gathered together against your holy servant Jesus, whom you anointed, both Herod and Pontius Pilate, along with the Gentiles and the peoples of Israel. . ."

According to these accounts, the local Jewish and Roman authorities, along with all the local people, Jew and Gentile alike, conspired against Jesus. However, their profession includes a surprise twist, when they explain that this happened in order "to do whatever your hand and your plan had predestined to take place." Satan, the Jews, and Gentiles, and those in authority may have worked together to perpetrate the greatest evil of all time; however, God's hand and Divine plan clearly governed the entire process. The end result made these well-known words of Jesus in John 3:16 possible. "For God so loved the world, that he gave his only Son, that whoever believes in him should not perish but have eternal life."

The evil of the crucifixion also shows us something surprising about the relationship between God and suffering. Doctor Who could have destroyed the Daleks, and forever rid the universe of their evil before they ever existed, but he chose not to. One of the results of that choice included eventually having to see his entire home world destroyed. He felt the same pain as other worlds, because of the Daleks. Similarly, God understands how it feels to experience evil the way we do, because He Himself experienced it when He took on human flesh. Tim Keller, pastor of Redeemer Presbyterian Church in New York City, put it this way:

> Yes, we don't know the reason God allows evil and suffering to continue, but we know what the reason isn't, what it can't be. It can't be that he doesn't love us! It can't be that he doesn't care. God so loved us and hates suffering that he was willing to come down and get involved in it.[23]

In conclusion, we can say that even if we don't know why evil exists, the fact that it does exist in no way negates God's goodness. Evil can serve a greater, redemptive purpose, even if we don't immediately know that purpose. Though we may not always know why we suffer at the hands of evil, we can know that God understands what this suffering feels like. We see all these principles most clearly demonstrated for us at the cross. And if we look closely, Scripture, history, and even *Doctor Who* can illuminate these truths for us.

ENDNOTES

1   ABC Nightline: *Face Off*. Original Air-Date March 26, 2009.
2   "Process Theology" and "Open Theism" fall under these categories. For a good critique, see Norman Geisler, *Creating God in the Image of Man?* (Ada, MI: Baker House Publishers, 1997).
3   Alvin Plantinga, *God, Freedom, and Evil* (Grand Rapids, MI: William B. Eerdmans Publishing Company, 1974), 10.
4   Nicholas Bunnin; E.P. Tsui-James, *The Blackwell Companion to Philosophy* (Hoboken, NJ: John Wiley & Sons, 2002), 481.
5   Louis Berkhof, *Systematic Theology* (London: Banner of Truth, 1949), 61.
6   As seen in "The Three Doctors", "The Five Doctors", "The Two Doctors", and "The Day of the Doctor".
7   A.W. Pink, *The Attributes of God* (Grand Rapids, MI: Baker House Books, 1975), 17.
8   David Herman; Manfred Jahn; Marie-Laure Ryan, *Routledge Encyclopedia of Narrative Theory* (New York, New York: Taylor & Francis, 2005), 442.
9   J.I. Packer, *Concise Theology: A Guide to Historic Christian Beliefs* (Wheaton, IL: Tyndale House Publishers, 1993), 36.
10   "Let's Kill Hitler."
11   "Genesis of the Daleks."
12   David J. Howe; Mark Stammers; Stephen James Walker, *Doctor Who: The Sixties* (London: Virgin Publishing, 1992), 31.
13   A title given to saints who had a huge impact on church doctrine.
14   Augustine, *Enchiridion*, III, 9.
15   Thomas Aquinas, 7 *Summa Theologica* Ia, q. 2, a. 3 ad 1; quoted on http://www.aquinasonline.com/Topics/probevil.html.
16   Dietrich Bonhoeffer, *Ethics*. (Fortress Press: Minneapolis, MN, 2005 reprint), 67.
17   Doctor Who: *The Day of the Doctor*. (Original Air-Date November 23, 2013).

18   "Dalek."
19   "The Waters of Mars."
20   Job 1.
21   Westminster Confession of Faith, V. 4.
22   Karl Barth, *Church Dogmatics IV-1* (London: T & T Clark, 1957), 246.
23   Tim Keller, *Service of Remembrance and Peace for 9-11 Victim's Families.* Ground Zero/St Paul's Chapel, New York, NY (Sep 10, 2006).

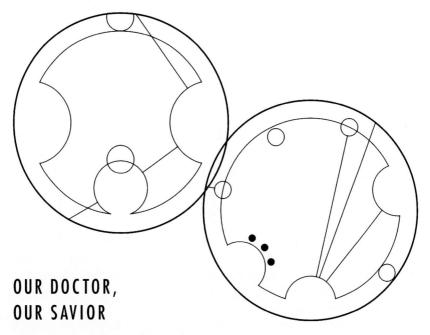

OUR DOCTOR,
OUR SAVIOR

SAVIOR: *Army of Ghosts/Doomsday*
ORIGINAL AIRDATE: JULY 1/8 2006

Throughout history, man has continually cried out for a savior. Watching the news each day shows our drastic situation: every corner of the globe is filled with war and poverty, crime and sadness, while our media is filled with depictions of different saviors, each trying desperately to make a difference. The cry for a savior spills into our imaginative literature, from Victor Hugo's *Les Miserables* to the dark streets of Batman's Gotham. Our world is sick, and it needs a Doctor.

I discovered *Doctor Who* just as David Tennant neared the end of his run as the Tenth Doctor, just prior to the airing of "The End of Time, Parts 1 & 2." The winter of 2009–2010 was one of the worst Ohio had in years, and the school I worked for had a full two weeks of snow days. Over those two weeks, at the urging of a close friend, I watched all four seasons of the new *Doctor Who*, and, with baited breath, I watched with the world as Tennant's time as the Tenth Doctor came to a close, with him telling us "I don't want to go."

In that closing line of the episode and the act of sacrifice that preceded it, the Doctor exemplified the savior figure. He sacrifices himself for the whole of the Earth, saving it from the clutches of evil Time Lords who seek to destroy it for their own benefit. This is the legacy of the Doctor, and rarely has there been a figure in pop culture who regularly demonstrates to the audience not merely the need for a hero, but the need for a savior. This savior does not, however, save us only from outside forces bent on death and destruction, but also from the ruination we humans continually and almost willingly bring upon ourselves.

Throughout the show's half-century of life, the Doctor places himself between humanity and harm, stating clearly that "It is defended," whatever the cost. At the close of Series 2, the Earth faces its greatest threat, caught in the crossfire between the Daleks and the Cybermen—both of whom desire the utter destruction of all life but their own. The two-part story, "Army of Ghosts" and "Doomsday," tells the tale of Rose Tyler's departure from the Doctor, as the Doctor sacrifices his happiness for the sake of humanity.

It would be easy to say that the Doctor's many death-regeneration cycles best exemplify his sacrifice, because those stories tell how he gives up his life. Yet when he comes back from his death he is a new man with a chance to remake himself, to establish new relationships. It is the loss of one of his best-loved companions that demonstrates the depths of his sacrifice. He must let Rose go in order that more people might live. His love for humanity as a whole outweighs the importance of his own happiness.

"Army of Ghosts" begins with the Doctor and Rose returning to Earth for a visit, yet as is always the case, something is amiss in England. When they return to Rose's flat, Rose's mother Jackie tells her that her grandfather will be stopping by for tea soon—but he has been dead for ten years. Just then, a spectral figure appears in the kitchen. These appearances are occurring worldwide, and no one is worried about it.

Jackie further mentions that she can smell the scent of her dead father's cigarettes when the ghost appears. Jackie and the world believe what they want to believe, regardless of the danger this puts them in. Rose counters Jackie, saying that she doesn't smell it. Jackie replies, "You've got to make an effort. You've got to want it, sweetheart." The Doctor perceives that "the more you want it the stronger it gets," which Jackie confirms. Whatever you want to be true is true—as long as you want it enough.

Humans are perfectly happy to pursue something completely unknown and potentially dangerous, but we tend to be blinded by our feelings—be they sentiment or greed. Jackie tells the Doctor and Rose that the planet panicked at first, but settled down, assuming that the forms must be ghosts, and sentient, and capable of thoughts and feelings of their own.[1] This speaks to man's desire to rationalize the irrational. The world says that truth is relative; it's what you want to believe, rather than something absolute. We are also told by the world to follow our hearts, the sources of wisdom that lead us to the greatest happiness.

Jackie desperately wants to think that her father has returned. She pleads:

"Think of it, though. All the people we've lost, families coming back whole. Don't you think it's beautiful?" The Doctor, unfazed by her emotion, firmly declares what is unpopular but true: "I think it's horrific."

Upon investigating the origins of the ghosts that have overtaken London, they discover that the Torchwood Institute is responsible for opening a hole in the fabric of Time and Space allowing the ghosts through. This is in the commendable hope of trying to tap an energy source that would reduce Britain's dependence on foreign oil, and yet they have forged ahead with very visible consequences. There are unknown creatures appearing across the globe, and still in the hopes of gaining a little more power, mankind is orchestrating its own destruction.

The Doctor brings another warning: he describes the spherical Void ship's purpose, how it's directly from Hell (the Void between Universes, outside Time and Space, a place of utter nothingness), and that it must contain something that needs to escape. Much like the arrival of the ghosts, all signs point to the eerie, disturbing nature of the Void ship. Heedless of his warning, Torchwood's immediate reaction is to crack open the thing which ripped a gash in the fabric of space and time. The Doctor is incredulous: "So, you find the breach, probe it, the sphere comes through six hundred feet above London, bam. It leaves a hole in the fabric of reality. And that hole, you think, oh, shall we leave it alone? Shall we back off? Shall we play it safe? Nah, you think let's make it bigger!"

In fact, they're so preoccupied with the brash discovery and scrutiny of the ghosts and the Void ship that they are oblivious to the dual incursions going on right under their noses. All too quickly, the Earth falls under the control of the Cybermen with little resistance, and the Daleks follow quickly after them. Humanity has given the Earth over to them simply by blindly pursuing their greed and pride. They have brought the enemy into the fold and welcomed them with open arms. By the time they realize their mistake, it is already too late. The Daleks and Cybermen both strive for domination of the Earth, and neither is afraid of the other. Without much effort, the Daleks begin to wipe out the Cybermen, and their war quickly catches humanity in the crossfire. Because of the humans' proud, indiscriminate pursuit of technological supremacy, they find themselves humbled in the most devastating way.

Fortunately, the Doctor sides with Earth against the tempest of mechanical destruction, despite mankind's myriad missteps. He persists in warning and saving humanity, despite mankind's dogged quest for self-destruction and disregard for the Doctor's aid. He has only ever helped humanity, cultivating a reputation for stepping in and saving the Earth countless times in his millennial existence, and yet they persist in betraying him again and again. This does not deter him, however. He pulls the universe back together, almost with his bare hands. He feels the sacrifice of this act more acutely than those he saves as he watches Rose Tyler disappear into another, unreachable dimension.

No matter our intentions, fallen humanity acts in a way that causes us to falter in our efforts and leads to us sabotaging ourselves. We cannot avoid the idols we embrace and the sin that like a vine wraps itself around us, causing us to stumble. That leads us to cry out for help like the Israelites in the book of Judges; this cycle will never cease. God describes how we always fall short of holiness. "The Lord looks down from heaven on the children of man, to see if there are any who understand, who seek after God. They have all turned aside; together they have become corrupt; there is none who does good, not even one."[2] In the absence of grace this can seem hopeless, but faith in the Christ who defeats every enemy gives us firm ground on which to stand. All the efforts based in our own strength fail, ripping holes in our universe—maybe not as literally as in *Doctor Who,* but the effects of those mistakes are all too real and can feel absolutely devastating.

We know that "the hearts of the children of man are full of evil, and madness is in their hearts while they live, and after that they go to the dead." Our sin is inherited through the fall, and we cannot undo it on our own. Without someone stepping in and rescuing us, we will drown in the mire of our own sin, for the consequence of our sin is a death we cannot avoid.[3] All of this does not, however, change the fact that God loves us when we do not deserve it and he never stops loving His children.

Mankind needs a savior, and we have needed that savior since the very first sin. The problem of pride and self-destruction is not a new one, nor is it reserved simply for the unchecked push of science beyond the boundaries of propriety. This hubris is at the very core of human nature; it is the plight of us all.

The Doctor steps into the midst of a war started by humanity's own deadly tendencies and puts an end to it. The soulless creatures felt no fear of one another or their prey, but the moment Rose mentions the Doctor's name, they halt in fear: "Five million Cybermen, easy. One Doctor? Now you're scared." In the same way, odds that are insurmountable to us are overcome by Christ's power. His love for us overwhelms our sins and their consequences. To humans, His children, God's protection and salvation are freely given. Why? He loves us.

Each of the Doctor's escapades since 2005 begins with the flight of the TARDIS through the Time Vortex—a tunnel of ever-shifting hues, lightning and imploding suns, an eternity of color and shape flashing by the hurtling TARDIS, heedless of the peril, for all that matters is the mission. The Doctor travels throughout time and space on his unrelenting mission to save humanity. Wherever he goes, he finds humans in trouble and in need of saving. Each time, without fail, he comes across humans who have gotten themselves in over their heads, either because of their own hubris or another aspect of their flawed human nature. Undaunted, he helps them anyway. It almost seems as though he planned it from the moment he stepped into his stolen TARDIS. He claims that he simply wants to explore the universe, but in reality he is looking after his adopted children: the human race. The TARDIS, its heart an independent, omniscient, omnipresent energy, has a mind of its own. Even when the Doctor wants nothing more than a vacation, the TARDIS takes him to where he is truly needed, sometimes stopping in a wholly unexpected place—but always in the right place.

We predict neither God's intentions nor His actions. Before time began, He set in motion his plan of redemption for humanity. No matter what mistakes we make, He will always work things out for our good and His glory.[4] No matter the situation, the Doctor is there to save humanity from itself, for he is a Time Lord, and he uses his powers for the good of others. Even more, God our Father is the Lord of Time, and before time began He established a plan for our redemption and ultimate salvation. He "chose us in him before the foundation of the world, that we should be holy and blameless before him. In love he predestined us for adoption as sons through Jesus Christ, according to the purpose of his will."[5] He established His grace before time began, before we were even trapped by our sins, and began a plan that would bring us back into His light. He called us to Him, and to His people. His grace is irresistible,[6] His sacrifice on the cross is cleansing, fully paying for our sins, allowing us to regenerate (in a more permanent way than the Doctor) as newly claimed creations.[7] We must repent and follow Christ in order to receive the full reward and justification of His gift of grace.[8] When this happens, we must turn away from our sins,[9] for no longer are we bound by the fetters of this world. When we falter, His grace is persistent in our lives. It remains so until beyond the end of Time,[10] when Heaven and Earth are reborn and renewed just as we are by His Grace.

The Doctor travels in and out of Time, saving those he comes across, and his salvation is irresistible and permanent. Often the people he meets have no idea of their peril; but he throws himself between them and danger, asking only that they trust him. And their encounters with the Doctor leave them changed. We often come across those whose lives he has touched, and they have been transformed, continuing the Doctor's work even when he is not physically beside them. His legacy lives on through them. Martha and Mickey become defenders of the universe;[11] Captain Jack, rogue turned hero, saves the Earth on a regular basis (though he has not necessarily turned from his sins—at all), and Sarah Jane Smith, despite being abruptly left on Earth by the Doctor, carried on his legacy by investigating and protecting the Earth from alien incursions.[12] The Doctor, like Christ, touches lives irrevocably. His salvation is persistent and full, and his followers are spread far and wide, testifying to his good name throughout time.[13]

Whenever the Doctor steps into a new adventure, he waxes poetic about humanity. He loves humans but acknowledges the many ways he has been let down by them. The Second Doctor confirms humanity's "favorite pastime of trying to destroy each other,"[14] while the Fourth Doctor admits, "It may be irrational of me, but human beings are my favorite species,"[15] even though your "ancestors have a talent for self-destruction." Even the lovable Fifth Doctor ponders the contradiction of loving something for no reason: "I sometimes wonder why I like the people of this miserable planet so much."[16] Each incarnation of the Doctor still cares deeply for humanity and works tirelessly for their protection.

Tennant's Doctor, more than any other, expresses this. Just after he awakes from his initial regeneration,[17] he promptly saves humanity from (another) terrible invasion. He praises them while protecting them:

> By the ancient rites of combat, I forbid you to scavenge here for the rest of time. And when go you back to the stars and tell others of this planet, when you tell them of its riches, its people, its potential. When you talk of the Earth, then make sure that you tell them this. It is defended […] Look at these people, these human beings. Consider their potential! From the day they arrive on the planet, blinking, step into the sun, there is more to see than can ever be seen, more to do than—no, hold on. Sorry, that's *The Lion King*. But the point still stands. Leave them alone!

John 3:16 assures us saying, "For God so loved the world, that he gave his only Son, that whoever believes in him should not perish but have eternal life." He intervenes on our behalf time and time again because He loves us, not because we have earned it. It is His love for us despite our penchant for failing Him; that makes His saving grace all the more meaningful; we don't deserve it.

The Doctor lauds humans' potential despite knowing full well the extent of their flaws. He claimed the title of the Champion of the Earth, fighting in hand-to-hand combat in defense of the Earth. He has incurred the wrath of at least two Queens of England, mortally drawn the Time Vortex into himself, combated werewolf-aliens, Cybermen, Daleks, Weeping Angels, Daemons, Sea-Devils, and Vampires, and thwarted the stubbornly recurring Master—all for our protection and care. But Christ's example is even more poignant, for He does what the Doctor cannot. The Doctor can save the Earth from some aliens and monsters, but Christ saved the world from Death, once and for all, and makes it possible for His people to live with Him in a new heavens and a new Earth beyond the end of Time.

ENDNOTES

1   Ironic, considering the fact that they're actually Cybermen who possess no human characteristics.
2   Psalm 14:2-3.
3   Romans 6:23.
4   Romans 8:28-31.
5   Ephesians 1:4-5.
6   John 6:44.
7   Titus 3:5.
8   Acts 2:38 ; Galatians 2:16-17.
9   Colossians 3:1-2.
10 Philippians 1:6.
11 "Torchwood."
12 "School Reunion."
13 "A Good Man Goes to War"; "Last of the Time Lords."
14 Patrick Troughton in "The Enemy of the World."
15 Tom Baker in "The Ark in Space."
16 Peter Davison in "Warriors of the Deep."
17 "The Christmas Invasion."

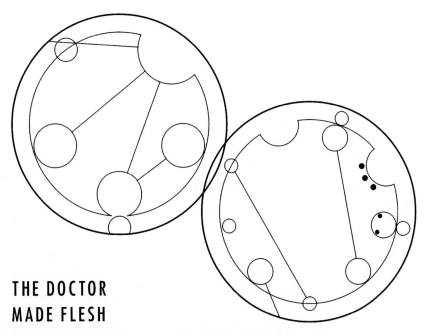

THE DOCTOR
MADE FLESH

INCARNATION: *Human Nature/The Family of Blood*
ORIGINAL AIRDATE: MAY 26/JUNE 2 2007

"And the Word became flesh, and dwelt among us..."[1]

"He's like fire and ice and rage. He's like the night, and the storm in the heart of the sun. He's ancient and forever. He burns at the center of time and he can see the turn of the universe. And... he's wonderful."[2]

The term *incarnation* represents the belief that the second person of the Trinity, "became flesh" by being conceived in the womb of Mary. Jesus took on a human body—truly becoming human when He was not already so—in order to facilitate the salvation of mankind. This is a fundamental theological teaching of Christianity It is also a fairly accurate description of the plot of the two-episode arc on *Doctor Who*, "Human Nature" and "The Family of Blood," in which the Doctor actually rearranges his biology through the use of a device called a Chameleon Arch, becoming human. That is, he's not merely masquerading as a human, as the device's name might imply, but rather the device actually facilitates its user's change from one species into another. This is not done lightly.

The Doctor chooses to employ it only because he feels it is the only way, also noting that, "it really hurts." And while the following several pages seek to explore parallels between Christ's Incarnation and the Doctor's transformation into a human being in these two episodes of *Doctor Who*, it is understood that these similarities were not intentionally designed to make the Doctor into a Christ-figure for our admiration. But stories are powerful things, and the one described here can, because of its setting and characters, illuminate our understanding of Christ's choice.

Among all possible alien species in the universe of *Doctor Who*, that the Doctor would choose to become human is not a huge surprise. Examples abound throughout the series, especially the reboot beginning in 2005, supporting the Doctor's love of humanity. And he loves humans, as God loves us, in spite of our flaws: "But God shows his love for us in that while we were still sinners, Christ died for us" [3]

While the Doctor always sees great potential in humanity, he chooses to be their protector, spending much of his time among them, in spite of them being at such an earlier stage of the intellectual development than his alien race, the Time Lords. In his fourth incarnation the Doctor says, "It might be irrational of me, but human beings are quite my favorite species."[4] The ninth incarnation of the Doctor takes that even further, indicating that not only does he like humans, but that an "ordinary man" is the most important thing in the universe.[5]

On the other hand, while the Doctor is full of love for humans, he is also fully cognizant of their flaws—much like God, who continually saves the Israelites throughout Exodus in spite of their lack of faith. When humans try to destroy the planet through the use of a mysterious device known as the Osterhagen Key rather than allow the human race to fall into enslavement by the Daleks, the Doctor chides them for the brutality of this solution and instructs one of his former Companions to make sure that the pieces of this plan are dismantled. Destruction of the human race isn't the answer, and you can hear the real anger in his voice when he learns of this plan.[6]

And in fact, the destruction of mankind, or at least a significant portion of it, is in a way the setting of the particular episodes under discussion here. "Human Nature" and "The Family of Blood" occur during the period immediately preceding World War I, the so-called "war to end all wars," when people were convinced because of the brutality of new weaponry that there was no way we would survive further wars going forward.

To consider how the Doctor's actions in these episodes reflect our understanding of the Incarnation, it would be useful to look at some of the attributes we also associate with God. And it is also useful to see how the Doctor's newfound humanity directly connects.

"Being human" is one of the themes of this two-episode arc, or rather, "what is it to be human?" is one of the questions the episodes pose through the plotline of the Doctor becoming one himself. We see the contrast between his Godlike knowledge and power as the Doctor, and the relatable flaws of his humanity as John Smith.

Consider what the Doctor gives up to be human. Once his biology is human and his Time Lord memory is erased (or at least hidden from him), he no longer has the vast knowledge of the universe that he once had. He has to muddle through life on limited information, not understanding the significance of many events unfolding around him. He has given up his near-omniscience.

The role he takes as a human being, however, is an academic one. He is a teacher at a school for boys. Even while he is not as nigh-omniscient as the Doctor, John Smith is a man who understands the value of learning. As he seeks to mentor and teach young men, he falls short because as a human he has flaws. He cannot see the truth about those who would harm and help him, but he nevertheless strives for the truth.

As a human, John Smith also gives up the Doctor's near-omnipotence. Within the science fiction world of *Doctor Who*, the Doctor is certainly not truly omnipotent, not in the sense that we think of when we contemplate God's infinite power. But he is so much more powerful than those around him, and therefore able to defeat any enemy, that he might as well be omnipotent from their point of view; he seems to them incapable of failing. John Smith, on the other hand, has none of that power. He is a human, weak and capable of being easily harmed, unable to do anything when confronted by the violence directed at him and those he cares for by the Family of Blood.

But again, as with John Smith's desire to learn, the episodes show him to be a person who understands the need for power and strength and someone who strives for it. As a teacher at the Farringham School for boys, where part of the boys' education includes weaponry and target practice in preparation for using such force in the war to come, John Smith assists the headmaster in instructing them in the art of warfare. He cannot match the power of the Doctor, but he displays an understanding for the necessity of it and tries to make sure he and his boys have enough to protect themselves. Of course, teaching them how to fight sets up an interesting contrast between the human John Smith and the near-omnipotent Doctor. The Doctor abhors violence and war.[7] He has seen that violence ultimately leads nowhere, and so he pursues non-violent solutions. John Smith, in his lack of understanding as a fallible human, does what he can to prepare the boys in his charge for a violent reality.

Goodness is another quality that the Doctor possesses in vast measure.[8] The show depicts him as (possibly) the ultimate good being in the universe. He constantly seeks to make things right when he can and to defeat evil, usually both at the same time. Similarly, John Smith tries to help the boys in his charge at Farringham School prepare for war. He tries to treat people well and practice justice, albeit on a much smaller scale.

The Doctor continually shows mercy to his enemies, in spite of the ease with which he could strike them down (and even in some cases in spite of a desire to do so). In "The Last of the Time Lords," the Doctor is elevated to an even more powerful position, and when faced with the opportunity to finally kill his archenemy, the Master, the Doctor instead holds the cowering man in his arms and tells him, "I forgive you."[9] And in the resolution of "Human Nature" and "The Family of Blood", the character of Baines (a schoolboy whose body was taken over by a member of the Family of Blood) explains "why this Doctor, who had fought with gods and demons, why he'd run away from us and hidden. He was being kind." So out of a great abundance of mercy, given his awesome and terrible powers, given the fact that he is, as schoolboy Tim Latimore tells us in the episode, "like the night, and the storm in the heart of the sun," the Doctor had chosen to hide and let the Family of Blood "off the hook," as it were, letting them die out on their own without harming anyone. But then their evil could no longer be tolerated, and he was forced to act. But his mercy and kindness extends as far as he can allow it to, until they force his hand with their destruction.

Again, like the Doctor, John Smith too shows mercy when he could choose not to do so. He is merciful to his students, recognizing his error in pushing them to fight the Family of Blood when they attack the school in search of the Doctor. Rather than allowing the boys to die fighting, he orders them to set down their guns and surrender in the hope that they might live.

The Doctor's life stretches on with no apparent end. In the fifty-plus year run of *Doctor Who*, his age has stretched to a length of over two thousand years. Because he can regenerate into a new body when the former one is damaged or infirm, and because the show and its owners will continue to give him new ways to do so as long as it is a profitable enterprise, he can indeed be nearly eternal, or as close as one can be without being a truly eternal God.

As a human being, John Smith's life is not eternal. He knows his life is finite and that he will die. In spite of this knowledge of his and every human's impending death, he strives for the eternal in ways that many of us do. When he is considering if he can remain John Smith or return to his true form as the Doctor, the audience sees a sort of flash-forward montage of images as he imagines what his human life would be. He marries his love, the school's nurse Joan Redfern, and they have children and grow old together. At the end of the montage, at the end of a long (human) life, he is concerned mostly about the lives of his children and grandchildren. Like all humans whose lives will end, we find our immortality through the continuation of our families, through our children. While John Smith cannot hope to live eternally, he can know that his legacy will live on through his children and their families.

Is the Doctor immutable, or does he change? The history of the program shows his physical change many times, but it goes to great pains to remind the audience that who the Doctor is, deep down inside, never changes. After he has transitioned into his twelfth incarnation, his Companion Clara—who has struggled throughout the episode with this changed physical appearance—gets a phone call literally from the past, from the Doctor she previously knew, the eleventh incarnation. At the conclusion of the phone call, the twelfth Doctor can tell that she is struggling with the fact that he looks different. He says to her, "You look at me and you can't see me. Have you any idea what that's like? I'm not on the phone. I'm right here, standing in front of you. Please just, just see me." What he's trying to say is that while his face and voice have changed, and while he seems much older to her now, he is still immutably the same man that he was before.[10]

John Smith is clearly not immutable. As a human man, it is not possible for him to be. But at the end of "The Family of Blood," when it is clear to him and to everyone else that he must stop being human and go back to being the Doctor, his desire is *not* to change. He mightily resists the call that he should return to his former, true self. But humans, unlike God, not only *do* change, but change is something we should embrace. We are born sinners and strive constantly not to be what we are. It is our flawed humanity that allows us— requires us even—to grow.

The punishment meted out by the Doctor to the Family of Blood as a result of their crimes shows that he has the character of God, that he is just. He has shown them mercy by choosing initially not to punish them. He gives them the chance to turn back from their evil deeds or to die in the course of their normal life spans without having done harm to others. But when they insist on doing harm to many, he must punish them, for he is just. And his punishment is not horrific; he does not kill them or do bodily harm. Instead, he imprisons them alive, forcing them to think about their crimes for eternity.

John Smith strives for justice, too. As he trains the boys of Farringham school for war, his motive is to preserve justice for his countrymen. Though his under- standing of the issues surrounding the march to world war in 1913 might be somewhat shallow and limited (given his perspective), the arc of his intent, as it were, bends toward justice.

The Doctor clearly possesses many traits in common with God. God is omni- scient and omnipotent; He is good and merciful; He is eternal and immutable; He is just and wise and infinite. But it is also clear that the human version of the Doctor, John Smith, strives toward all of these ideals. It is clear he can never reach them, at least not at the level that the Doctor does. But as a human, he understands them even without the Doctor's power or experiences.

What does this tell us about what it is to be human? What does it mean for God to become man, and what does it mean for man to become a son of God?

Perhaps being human is to always be striving for ideals that we can never achieve without God's help, and to understand that because we are made in the image of God, we are already who we are intended to be, possessing His qualities in smaller measures.

As John Smith is a human made in the image of the deified version of himself, the nearly all-powerful all-knowing Doctor, so are we as humans made in the image of our God, struggling toward an ideal we can never reach without the intervention of Christ's crucifixion, but built with the desire to be the definitive versions of ourselves, the version God intended us to be when He created us in His image.

One way to discuss the Incarnation is to consider it in this way, from the standpoint of what makes us human and what makes God who He is. But the Incarnation can't be considered without also contemplating the critical element of sacrifice.

God sacrificed His son, allowing Jesus to take human form, knowing He would experience the violence visited on him by taking on the sins of humanity. And Jesus sacrificed Himself in order to do this.

From the human perspective, there is sacrifice as well. When Jesus became a man, he emptied himself of His Godlike-ness, though he didn't lose his spirituality. Likewise, the Doctor glorifies what it is to be human. He so clings to John Smith's humanity that, at the end, when it becomes apparent that he must become the Doctor again or everyone will die, he realizes what he'd be giving up. The brief but poignant montage (referenced above) shows his human life with his family, and it is hard to look at this and not understand that he is making a sacrifice to be the godlike being he normally is. The Doctor knows he cannot be in a typical human relationship, as he explained earlier in the series to Rose:

DOCTOR: I don't age. I regenerate. But humans decay. You wither and you die. Imagine watching that happen to someone who you—
ROSE: What, Doctor?
DOCTOR: You can spend the rest of your life with me, but I can't spend the rest of mine with you. I have to live on. Alone. That's the curse of the Time Lords.[11]

His life span is nearly infinite compared to a human's, and so, to avoid the pain he has experienced when human Companions die, he chooses not to try to act like he can be human. In this montage, though, because he is at that moment human, he entertains the notion for a short time, and the glimpse into that potential future is hard for him to relinquish.

Relinquish it he does, however, after being encouraged to by the humans around him. Martha Jones (his then current Companion) knows that he must be the Doctor again if the world is to be saved. The motives of Joan Redfern, the human with whom he has fallen in love, are more complicated. A widow who never expected to find love again, she is disappointed to learn that her new love is not who she thought he was. And she is not attracted to the Doctor and what he represents at all. But she knows that he must return to that role, and she helps the human John Smith find the strength to do it despite his fear and reluctance. She, too, sacrifices something in this transition. Whereas Martha is attracted to everything that the Doctor represents, Joan yearns to be with a man who is human and who embraces his humanity and all the limitations and joys that come with that.

So we see in John Smith a fully human man with all the potential frailties of a human who nevertheless chooses to embrace the trial ahead of him in spite of his fear, in order to save humanity. It is hard not to see Christ in this character, at least in part, especially when we look to Christ's prayer at Gethsemane: "My Father, if it be possible, let thus cup pass from me; nevertheless, not as I will, but as you will."[12] We see in this prayer a Christ who, though He will choose to do the Father's will, is struggling with the trial to come.

There are many examples in this two-episode arc and the series as a whole that help to illustrate the points made here. And yet there are many contrasting examples that separate the story from our understanding of the Incarnation of Christ. Whereas Jesus Christ is the perfect human and succeeds as one in every way, John Smith, our representative human in this story, fails in many ways. He succumbs to the racism and warlike violence of his time, and he fears what will become of him if he allows himself to be transformed back into the Doctor. But "Human Nature" and "The Family of Blood" are not, collectively, trying to communicate an orthodox version of the Incarnation for their audience. So what value do we find in looking at these similarities while acknowledging the many differences necessitated by the ongoing storyline of a long-running series with established characters? The value is that it helps us to imagine in a new way what it looks like for a divine (or, in this case, nearly divine) being to empty himself of power and embrace becoming fully human. And it also helps us to see (by looking through the eyes of John Smith and Joan Redfern) how wonderful it is to be truly human.

ENDNOTES

1   John 1:14.
2   "Human Nature."
3   Romans 5:8.
4   "The Ark in Space."
5   "Father's Day."
6   "Journey's End."
7   In part, because of the destruction wrought by others and himself as The War Doctor (The Sontarans told legends of the Doctor leading Time Lords into battle) during The Last Great Time War between the Time Lords and the Daleks. It lasted for at least 400 years, however, it was fought throughout countless time periods so it seemed to last much longer. On the last day of the Time War the Dalek fleets surrounded Gallifrey and captured the city of Arcadia, then laid siege to the capital itself. The War Doctor stole an ancient Gallifreyan weapon known as The Moment and destroyed Gallifrey in order to wipe out the Daleks. But not really. *Spoilers!* Although the Doctor is racked with guilt for destroying Gallifrey, in reality, The Moment helped 13 incarnations of the Doctor to gather to save Gallifrey by freezing it in time in a pocket universe. In the wake of the sudden disappearance of Gallifrey, the Daleks accidentally annihilated themselves.
8   Although throughout Season 8 he is haunted by the question, "Am I a good man?" The season concludes with the Doctor concluding: "I am not a good man! And I'm not a bad man. I am not a hero. I'm definitely not a president. And no, I'm not an officer. You know what I am? I . . . am . . . an idiot. With a box and a screwdriver, passing through, helping out, learning."
9   "The Last of the Time Lords."
10   "Deep Breath."
11   "School Reunion."
12   Matthew 26:39.

...FOREVER
AND EVER. AMEN.

PRAYER: *The Girl in the Fireplace*
ORIGINAL AIRDATE: MAY 6, 2006

> *"...we are Gods ambassadors and image bearers, charged with caring for creation, [therefore] we bring to him the concerns of creation, praying for each other, for the church, and for the world;"*
> —*James K.A. Smith,* Desiring the Kingdom

> *"Prayer can be simple, but it's not easy. Nothing great is."*
> —*Tim Keller*

I remember first watching *Doctor Who* as a child, late at night on PBS. Jon Pertwee was my first Doctor, and Elisabeth Sladen was my first Companion. The television show was a solitary pleasure and therefore none of my friends had any idea why I eventually asked my grandmother to knit a ridiculously long scarf for me. The series was quite entertaining, and I found it began to have an affect on me. In addition to birthing an obsession with cricket sweaters, it worked on my imagination. It made me think about things that had never before crossed my mind. For example, might mummies actually be robots, and sarcophagi be space-time tunnels?[1] Or might the Loch Ness monster have been a cyborg weapon of the Zygons instead of an old land-locked dinosaur as I had once assumed?[2] And was Time a stream through which one could travel in a blue police phone box?

At some point (not long after the Doctor began wearing a celery stick on his lapel) my pastor began to work on my imagination within the realm of theology. He made me think about things that had never before crossed my mind. Ideas such as God being outside of Time, exercising His sovereignty by foreordaining and predestining events in people's lives. At that time, such ideas were akin to science fiction to me. You might imagine my surprise when he revealed to me that these concepts had been in plain sight in the Bible throughout my entire life.

Zygons and Predestination were new ideas to me, but Prayer is a concept that has been a fixed point in my mind for as long as I can remember. Prayer is a means of grace given to us by God through which we enter into communion with Him and grow in Him. Prayer includes praise, thanksgiving, confession, supplication, and intercession with God. Sinclair Ferguson wrote that prayer is where we "ask God to accomplish what He has promised in His Word.... [Christians] go to Him, as children do to a loving human father. They know that if they can say to an earthly father, 'But, father, you promised....,' they can both persist in asking and be confident that he will keep his word."[3] I've struggled over the years doubting many things, but I've always firmly believed that my heavenly Father keeps His word. Therefore I pray with confidence, knowing that God hears me and will give to me what I ask, for my good, and according to His will.[4]

My prayer life was shaped by the Lord's Prayer (with most of my particular prayers consisting of elaborations on what I wanted God to understand I saw as coming under the category of my "daily bread") and *The Book of Common Prayer.*[5] My grandfather was the pastor of our church when I was young, and to this day I still can almost mimic his cadence when I read the General Thanksgiving. Using that book taught me to pray for Peace, Grace, Forgiveness, Civil Authorities, Aid against All Perils, the Impenitent, and much more. But how do those various prayers work if God is sovereign over all things and exists outside of Time and Space?

When concepts like Prayer and Sovereignty crash, sometimes it takes the Doctor to work it all out. An essay on Prayer and *Doctor Who* could focus on the silly moment when, following the epic missionary journey Martha Smith undertook to evangelize the Earth, the whole world prays—err, that is, creates a "telepathic field" with the Doctor.[6] But instead, let us take a look at the episode that brought me back to the show, following Peter Davidson's tour of duty as the Doctor.

"The Girl in the Fireplace" is the fourth episode of Series Two, written by Steven Moffat. It won the 2007 Hugo Award for Best Dramatic Presentation, Short Form. In that episode, the Doctor, Rose Tyler, and Mickey Smith land the

TARDIS on an abandoned spaceship in the fifty-first century—two and a half galaxies from Earth in the Diagmar Cluster. The Doctor and his companions explore the ship and find an eighteenth century French fireplace on board. And, the fireplace is double sided. One side is in the spaceship with them and one side is in France. The fireplace is a doorway through space and Time (or, "a spatio-temporal hyperlink" as the Doctor decides to call it). Looking in the fireplace, the Doctor sees a young girl, named Reinette.[7] The Doctor presses a hidden button on the mantle, causing the fireplace to rotate like some mysterious bookcase in an episode of *Scooby-Doo, Where Are You!* or Batgirl's secret revolving wall that hid her Batgirl Cycle in the '60s *Batman* TV series. Suddenly, the Doctor finds himself in Reinette's bedroom, in Paris, in 1727. But while the Doctor had stepped almost immediately through the opening in Time, the girl informs him that it has been months since they last spoke. A clockwork android wearing eighteenth century clothing and a jester's mask leads the Doctor back through the fireplace. Moments later, the Doctor returns to Reinette's bedroom and discovers that she is now a young woman. At the end of their meeting the Doctor deduces that she will one day be Madame de Pompadour, the mistress of King Louis XV.

Back again through the fireplace, the Doctor finds that Rose and Mickey have wandered off, in spite of having been under strict instructions. "[I]t's rule one. Don't wander off. I tell them, I do. Rule one. There could be anything on this ship." While searching for his Companions, the Doctor finds a horse[8] who has slipped through one the many "gateways to history" that have been opened from the ship into various moments in the life of Reinette. The Doctor proceeds to use these openings to step into Reinette's life to spy on her, dance with her, and protect her from the clockwork androids. During one of his visits, the Doctor even invents the banana daiquiri—a few centuries early. Toward the end of the episode (well, and also at the beginning) Madame de Pompadour calls through the fireplace: "Are you there? Can you hear me? I need you now. You promised. The clock on the mantel is broken. It is time. Doctor! Doctor!" Of course, the Doctor comes—in the nick of time—and saves her from being decapitated by clockwork androids.

What does all this have to do with prayer? "The Girl in the Fireplace" could be seen as a parable for persistence in prayer along the lines of the Persistent Widow found in Luke 18. When Madame de Pompadour calls out in desperate need to her Gallifreyan god, she trusts that he will do as he has promised, and come to her rescue in her time of greatest need.[9] But that is not the central concern of this essay, and even if persistence in prayer was the theme, a short reflection on into prayer is in order.

What is prayer? Question 98 of the Westminster Shorter Catechism declares that prayer is "an offering up of our desires unto God, for things agreeable to his will, in the name of Christ, with confession of our sins, and thankful acknowledgment of his mercies." This is a good and thorough definition as would be expected from the Westminster Shorter Catechism. Another definition for prayer states that "prayer is the divinely appointed means through which we commune with the living God and advance his kingdom."[10] What is helpful about such a definition is that it poetically captures both the intimate aspect of relationship and enjoyment of God along with the ongoing redemptive work of Christ. Along with prayer having purpose, in the Bible we're also taught that prayer has form. There is a pattern for prayer laid out for us by Jesus in Matthew 6.[11] Whether it is individual or corporate, prescribed or extemporaneous, silent or shouted, prayer generally consists of four elements: adoration and praise of God, confession of sin and requests for forgiveness, thanks for good gifts received, and petitions for our needs and the needs of others. Usually our prayers bottom out as whining petitions for whims and novelties; it is as if the sum of the Christian life consists in merely sitting on the lap of a cosmic Santa Claus and reading down out of fancies: peace and prosperity, health and happiness, love and respect, safety and sonic screwdrivers. But Tim Keller urges followers of Christ to offer gospel-centered prayer, rather than anxious laundry lists. He writes,

> Our desires are always idolatrous to some degree, and when we pray without dealing with that first, we find our prayers only make us more anxious. Instead, we should always say, in effect, "Lord, let me see your glory as I haven't before; let me be so ravished with your grace that worry and self-pity and anger and indifference melt away!" Then, when we turn to ask God for admission to grad school or healing of an illness, those issues will be put in proper perspective. We will say, "Lord, I ask for this because I think it will glorify you—so help me get it, or support me without it." If the overall focus of the prayer is on God's glory and the gospel, our individual petitions will be made with great peace and confidence.[12]

Prayer is God's design for working out God's designs. As such, in God's great plan for Life, the Universe, and Everything, He has been pleased to allow prayer to be key to battlefield victories (Exodus 17:8-13), stop rain (1 Kings 18:41-45), loose chains and open prison doors (Acts 12:1-17), raise the dead (Acts 9:40), and prayer will even usher in the close of history at the end of Time (Rev. 8:1-5). Prayer is offered by those who belong to Christ and for his sake. We are to pray in the Spirit, that is, in fellowship with Him and in line with His works. This is done by allowing our prayers to be "instructed by Scripture, structured by Scripture, and saturated in Scripture."[13] We know that "our prayers depend on no merit of our own, but all their worth and hope of success are founded and depend on the promises of God."[14] We pray by faith, believing God hears and responds. James gives us an example of God responding to the prayers of a person just like us (though certainly not an ordinary man) in the fifth chapter of his Epistle: "Elijah was a man with a nature like ours, and he prayed fervently that it might not rain, and for three years and six months it did not rain on the earth. Then he prayed again, and heaven gave rain, and the earth bore its fruit."

Some may balk at the idea of a God who can change weather patterns while others think such a God wouldn't bother to listen. "An infinite-personal God is such an astounding idea that we struggle to grasp it. Our modern world is okay with an infinite God, as long as he doesn't get too personal . . . Non-Western cultures have no trouble thinking that God is personal but they doubt he is infinite."[15] But the Bible asserts both, as in Isaiah 57:15:

> For thus says the One who is high and lifted up,
>   who inhabits eternity, whose name is Holy:
> "I dwell in the high and holy place,
>   and also with him who is of a contrite and lowly spirit,
> to revive the spirit of the lowly,
>   and to revive the heart of the contrite."

God dwells *both* in the high and holy place *and* with the lowly spirit.

In the Gospels we learn to call out to this infinite-personal God, and pray " . . . Thy Kingdom come." As Winston Churchill calls the Doctor at the end of an episode and says, "Tricky situation, Doctor. Potentially very dangerous. I think I'm going to need you,"[16] and so we call out to God to express our need. We want Him to come bring hope, order, and goodness. And we want Him to bring them not to some other time and space, but now—to *our* time and space. Space, or Place, is a very important component of the way God works in prayer.

Jesus' teaching on prayer centers on our urgent dependence on God. Prayer is *asking*. Prayer is a request. And since it is a request, it may or may not be granted. C.S. Lewis reminds us that "if an infinitely wise Being listens to the requests of finite and foolish creatures, of course He will sometimes grant and sometimes refuse them."[17] In addition to denying the requests of foolish people, He will even refuse prayers offered by perfect people, as in Gethsemane. But still, Jesus presses us to ask:

> "Which of you who has a friend will go to him at midnight and say
> to him, 'Friend, lend me three loaves, for a friend of mine has arrived on
> a journey, and I have nothing to set before him'; and he will answer from

within, 'Do not bother me; the door is now shut, and my children are with me in bed. I cannot get up and give you anything'? I tell you, though he will not get up and give him anything because he is his friend, yet because of his impudence he will rise and give him whatever he needs. And I tell you, ask, and it will be given to you; seek, and you will find; knock, and it will be opened to you. For everyone who asks receives, and the one who seeks finds, and to the one who knocks it will be opened. What father among you, if his son asks for a fish, will instead of a fish give him a serpent; or if he asks for an egg, will give him a scorpion? If you then, who are evil, know how to give good gifts to your children, how much more will the heavenly Father give the Holy Spirit to those who ask him!"[18]

Clearly, as followers of Christ, earnest prayer is our duty and our privilege. And in an essay on prayer in a book about *Doctor Who,* "we must carefully attend to the circumstance of Time" as John Calvin has said. The famous theologian urges the Christian that although we should pray without ceasing, yet, due to our weakness (such as our "torpor") we should appoint "special hours for this exercise, hours which are not to pass away without prayer," specifically:

. . . when we rise in the morning, before we commence our daily work, when we sit down to food, when by the blessing of God we have taken it, and when we retire to rest. This, however, must not be a superstitious observance of hours, by which, as it were, performing a task to God, we think we are discharged as to other hours; it should rather be considered as a discipline by which our weakness is exercised, and ever and anon stimulated. In particular, it must be our anxious care, whenever we are ourselves pressed, or see others pressed by any strait, instantly to have recourse to him not only with quickened pace, but with quickened minds; and again, we must not in any prosperity of ourselves or others omit to testify our recognition of his hand by praise and thanksgiving. Lastly, we must in all our prayers carefully avoid wishing to confine God to certain circumstances, or prescribe to him the time, place, or mode of action. In like manner, we are taught by this prayer not to fix any law or impose any condition upon him, but leave it entirely to him to adopt whatever course of procedure seems to him best, in respect of method, time, and place. For before we offer up any petition for ourselves, we ask that his will may be done, and by so doing place our will in subordination to his, just as if we had laid a curb upon it, that, instead of presuming to give law to God, it may regard him as the ruler and disposer of all its wishes.[19]

Therefore, according to Calvin's convictions, we are to have special times to pray—not tell God what time He should act on our prayers or how in Time He should act on our prayers. But how can God accomplish his eternal purposes through our time-locked prayers? J.I. Packer says,

> There is no tension or inconsistency between the teaching of Scripture on God's sovereign foreordination of all things and on the efficacy of prayer. God foreordains the means as well as the end, and our prayer is foreordained as the means whereby he brings his sovereign will to pass.[20]

John Calvin urges his readers to hold in tension both the spontaneous course of God's providence and God's responsiveness to our prayers, insisting that "our prayers are anticipated by Him in His freedom, yet, what we ask we gain by prayer."[21] We must remember that God is not in Time. C.S. Lewis asserts that "if our prayers are granted at all they are granted from the foundation of the world. God and His acts are not in time. Intercourse between God and man occurs at particular moments for the man, but not for God."[22]

It is difficult to wrap your head around such disparate concepts as God working out His will *before* Time and our prayers in Time being effectual. It is at this point that it is helpful to return to *Doctor Who*. Although the analogy is certainly limited, "The Girl in the Fireplace" can be of assistance. Towards the climax of that episode, Rose enters France in the 1700's through an opening behind a large tapestry. She had been sent by the Doctor to warn Madame de Pompadour of a dangerous event that would be coming in about five years time. She fumbles a bit, trying to explain time travel and space ships to an eighteenth century french mistress. Reinette cuts through it all and summarizes Rose's explanation in this way: "There is a vessel in your world where the days of my life are pressed together like the chapters of a book, so that he may step from one to the other without increase of age while I, weary traveler, must always take the slower path."

From Reinette's perspective, life on board the spaceship is timeless. She and the king of France both observed that the Doctor does not appear to age. The Doctor and his companions seemed to be able to step in and out of any moment along "the slower path." In the same way, we find ourselves on the slower path. The days of our lives unfold like a book, and the chapters spread out in Time. We may pray in "Chapter 1" of our life or in "Chapter 21," but both prayers reach God at the same moment—the timelessness of Eternity. Again, God is not in Time. In a way, God hears my prayer and my grandfather's prayer together, at the same instant. Parenthetically, it follows that, although years apart from my perspective, my death and my grandfather's death occur at the same "time." We both leave the limits and constraints of Time and enter into Eternity together at the Final

Judgment, walking together into the New Jerusalem on the New Earth.[23]

Without a doubt, this is all wibbly-wobbly, timey-wimey stuff. "Trying to dissect how prayer works is like using a magnifying glass to try to figure out why a woman is beautiful."[24] And trying to use an episode of *Doctor Who* to explain how prayer works is equally ridiculous. All we can really know is that in some mysterious way our finite prayers are used by God in His continuous act of carrying out His goals throughout all of Time and Space, for His own glory. The thoughtful Whovian (or philosophical Determinist) may assert that prayer is useless since God is outside of Time and ask, "Does He not know without a monitor both what our difficulties are, and what is meet for our interest, so that it seems in some measure superfluous to solicit Him by our prayers, as if He were winking, or even sleeping, until aroused by the sound of our voice?"[25] But C.S. Lewis challenges this thinking when he writes, "I suppose you never ask the man next to you to pass the salt, because God knows best whether you ought to have salt or not. And I suppose you never take an umbrella, because God knows best whether you ought to be wet or dry."[26] Reason may claim that all of this is absurd. Reason tells you prayer cannot work. But as the Doctor said, "Oh pffft— you never want to listen to reason."

Prayer challenges our post-Enlightenment arrogance and brings us to a place humility. In prayer we are entirely dependent. But this lowly state of dependency is not a curse, but instead it is a glorious calling. We are called to pray to the omnipotent maker of Time. Indeed, prayer banks on God "transcending the confines of place and time, and as the Creator of the universe, being interested and concerned about concrete realities that face us here in our finitude."[27] And we are called to pray all kinds of prayers—supplications, intercessions, and thanksgivings—for all people, for it is good, and it is pleasing in the sight of God."[28] Prayer is good, and regardless of the outcome, it is good for us. As we follow the "slow path" prayer shapes us and forms us. And while we are being molded through prayer we are comforted to know that we are not calling out to empty space. Our Father sits outside of Time on His throne in Heaven, but like the Prodigal Son's father He is always looking for us. He is always present in our Present. And when we call out in humble desperation, God comes and saves us—just as He promised.

ENDNOTES
1   "Pyramids of Mars."
2   "Terror of the Zygons ."
3   Sinclair Ferguson, In Christ Alone - excerpt: http://www.ligonier.org/blog/prayer-faith/
4   Mark 11:24, Matthew 7:7, etc.
5   That is, the 1928 Book of Common Prayer as used by The Reformed Episcopal Church (REC).
6   "Last of the Time Lords."

7   Jeanne Antoinette Poisson (December 29, 1721–April 15, 1764), known as Reinette ("little queen") to her friends.
8   Arthur . . . a good name for a horse.
9   He has watched over me my whole life and he will not desert me tonight."
10 Stanley D. Gale, *Why Do We Pray? Basics of the Faith* (Phillipsburg: NJ, P&R Publishing, 2012), 7.
11 Another helpful form is the famous Jesus Prayer. An expanded, trinitarian version of that prayer reads:

> Father almighty, maker of heaven and earth:
> Set up your kingdom in our midst.
> Lord Jesus Christ, Son of the living God:
> Have mercy on me, a sinner.
> Holy Spirit, breath of the living God:
> Renew me and all the world.

—http://ntwrightpage.com/Wright_Prayer_Trinity.htm.

Or consider the form of a prayer of Saint Benedict (480–547 AD):

> Gracious and holy Father, please give me:
> Intellect to understand you;
> Reason to discern you; Diligence to seek you;
> Wisdom to find you; A spirit to know you;
> A heart to meditate upon you;
> Ears to hear you;Eyes to see you;
> A tongue to proclaim you;
> A way of life pleasing to you;
> Patience to wait for you;
> and Perseverance to look for you.

12 http://www.redeemer.com/r/prayer_and_the_gospel/
13 Gale, *Why Do We Pray?*, 11.
14 John Calvin, *Institutes of the Christian Religion*, Chapter 20 "Of Prayer—A Perpetual Excercise of Faith. The Daily Benefits Derived From It.," Section 14.
15 Paul E. Miller, *A Praying Life: Connecting with God in a Distracting World* (Carol Stream, IL: NavPress, 2009), 114.
16 "The Beast Below."
17 C.S. Lewis, *The World's Last Night and Other Essays* (New York: Mariner Books, 1959), 4.
18 Luke 11:5–13.
19 John Calvin, Institutes of the Christian Religion, Chapter 20 "Of Prayer—A Perpetual Excercise of Faith. The Daily Benefits Derived From It.," Section 50.
20 J.I. Packer, *Concise Theology: A Guide to Historic Christian Beliefs* (Wheaton, IL: Tyndale House Publishers, 1993), 189.
21 John Calvin, *Calvin's Commentaries, A Harmony of the Gospels Matthew, Mark and Luke, Vol. III,* (Edinburgh: Saint Andrew's Press, 1975), 204.
22 C.S.Lewis, *Letters to Malcolm: Chiefly on Prayer* (London: Geoffrey Bles Ltd, 1964), 69.
23 That is, the new heavens and new earth promised in Scripture. Not to be confused, of course, with the New Earth in the M87 galaxy, introduced in the April 2006 episode of *Doctor Who.*
24 Miller, *A Praying Life, 128.*
25 John Calvin, *Institutes of the Christian Religion*, Chapter 20 "Of Prayer—A Perpetual Excercise of Faith. The Daily Benefits Derived From It.," Section 3.
26 C. S. Lewis, *God in the Dock* (Grand Rapids, MI: Wm. B. Eerdmans Publishing, 1972), 217.
27 James K.A. Smith, *Desiring the Kingdom (Cultural Liturgies): Worship, Worldview, and Cultural Formation* (Orlando, FL: Baker Press, 2009).
28 28 1 Timothy 2:1–5

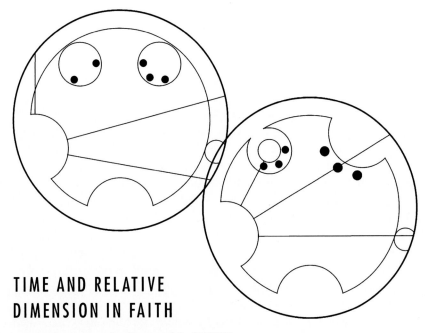

TIME AND RELATIVE
DIMENSION IN FAITH

FAITH: *Journey to the Center of the TARDIS*
ORIGINAL AIRDATE: APRIL 27, 2013

> *"It's called the TARDIS. It can travel anywhere in time and space. And it's mine.... Go on. Say it. Most people do."*[1]

> *"Oh, the depth of the riches and wisdom and knowledge of God! How unsearchable are his judgments and how inscrutable his ways!"*[2]

As a pastor I'm always trying to engage with our present world to bring the unchangeable truth of the gospel of Christ to a new audience "that they may be saved."[3] I am always on the lookout for contemporary metaphors that will help me do that.[4] This essay aims to share with the reader some of the metaphors found in the TARDIS, and bring together Whovian quotes and Scripture, as above.

I was reminiscing with friends in 2013 (the fiftieth anniversary of *Doctor Who*) how we genuinely *did* hide behind the sofa when it was screened. We were scared to watch, but we had to stay in the room for fear of not finding out what was going to happen! We were only six or seven years old at the time. So when the BBC showed again—late at night and back-to-back—all four episodes of the very first story, "An Unearthly Child," I was given the service address for my Christmas school assembly and Midnight Communion: the incarnate Christ, the most unearthly child there has ever been. I had my engaging metaphor. Only fifteen minutes into the first ever episode, and we are introduced to the inside of a key "character"—the TARDIS—with a foretaste of all that followed in the next fifty years as "her" character develops.

Having genuinely thanked God for the idea, and for the blessing of my own time machine in the shape of a DVD recorder, I watched all four episodes (barely 25 minutes each in those days). I can see why, as children, we found it so scary: candles inside skulls, skeletons, dark shadows, and creepy music (despite the polystyrene props and poorly faked Neolithic animals).[5]

Having also trained as a scientist,[6] I find I'm always aware of the world around me, and constantly making sense of it by the metaphors science has given me. But also working to make sense of it from God's perspective, in the metaphors He has given me in Scripture. I find this an invaluable match to help me to move people from a solely scientific and mechanistic world view to one that engages with the reality of a living and active God who loves us and his *kosmos* deeply.[7] One of the things for which the Doctor uses his TARDIS is to engage meaningfully with sentient creatures using its universal translation circuit, and similarly one of the key factors about engaging with any culture is knowing its world view and finding hooks to engage its thinking in order to lead it into faith in Christ, or to take believers deeper into Christ.

MY RELATIONSHIP WITH SCIENCE AND FAITH

There have been essentially four historic approaches to science and faith: *conflict, independent, dialogue* and *integrative*.[8]

In the caricature of *conflict*, both scientist and cleric dig trenches of dogmatic viewpoints from which they lob grenades of abuse and scorn at one another. The truth is often not so extreme, but there are still some scientists who are determined to debunk religion from reductionist and mechanistic viewpoints,[9] and Christians who are ardent fundamentalists try to trivialize science.[10] Sadly, this approach puts the Church in a bad light for its mission.[11]

In the *independent* family of approaches, there are several nuances on a theme, but essentially they all take the view that science and theology address different spheres of life and so do not need to be in conflict, but just exist side by side.[12] Whilst this approach is better than conflict, it gives those who hold a modern scientific world view the message that faith is irrelevant to *real* life. This is the kind of view the majority of the ruling Time Lords took at the very start of *Doctor Who*—looking on, but not engaging with the lives of the species they watched.

In *dialogue*, there is recognition by both science and theology that the other exists, and that they have helped each other's development historically. There is broad engagement at a philosophical level, but not in any detailed theory. Most individuals who take this approach are deeper-thinking scientists or theologians, but few appear to be both.[13]

As both a scientist and as a believer and disciple of Christ, I prefer the *integrative* approach, which lays hold of specific theories of both science and theology and wrestles with them. Many who take this approach are both scientists and theologians, like Peacocke.[14] For him God "transcends the world but is immanent in the world . . . [rather than a world] interrupted by gaps in which God alone operates."[15] This is the approach I take here, since I consider it gives a genuine edge to the mission of the church through being seen as engaging and relevant. It is also helpful to note that the Doctor engages deeply with every new culture he encounters, and not just with the technological aspects of time travel, which is why he fell out with the ruling Time Lords and ran off in the TARDIS to help those cultures.

It should be stated that any models of science, theology, or the two combined, are just that—they are models: pictures and descriptions of a reality that we cannot visualize, in terms of things that we can. For example, we cannot *see* an atom but we can represent it mathematically and think of it as a nucleus with electrons orbiting it. Likewise, Christ's atonement can be visualized as a ransom which is paid to buy us back for our sin. The reality of both, for believers at any rate, is indisputable yet it is far greater and lies beyond the model.[16][17]

Doctor Who is all great stuff, and ranks up there with the best of science fiction or science fantasy. I view it under the banner, as it were, of my integrative approach—taking up the metaphors presented me in the series so as to find significant and, I hope, useful parallels of the fantasy of *Doctor Who* in our genuine reality of life and faith.

INTEGRATING THEOLOGY AND THE TARDIS

Take out your TARDIS key[18] and let us begin our investigation of that famous blue box. On our tour of the TARDIS, we will visit the Engine Room, the Library, the Console Room, and more, considering specific properties of the TARDIS and linking them with the deep questions of "life, the universe, and everything."[19]

IT'S BIGGER ON THE INSIDE![20]

One concept that I dearly love about the TARDIS, particularly with my scientific understanding of time and space, is that it is so much bigger on the inside, but "normal" on the outside. In *Journey to the Centre of the TARDIS*[21] you get to see how much, *much* bigger it is inside until, eventually, you reach the centre of the TARDIS. We shall explore some of these aspects later on, but for now, let's stick with this major fact.[22]

As within the depths of the TARDIS we find passages, rooms, and hidden places, so we can plumb the depths of God, exploring literally, passages of Scripture, the different rooms of prayer, the gems of wisdom hidden away in places for us to discover as "in Him, we live and move and have our being"[23] and ultimately come to reach the centre of God, and meet Him face to face.[24] He is the eternal sanctuary in whom we can hide and be rescued in our circumstances and, indeed, from our very selves.

I turn from Sci-Fi back to reality to discover the one "through whom also He [God] created the world."[25] The Greek word there for *world* in Hebrews 1 conveys the thought of both Time and Space—where we get our English word *aeon*. We find that the one through whom God made the universe in which we live, becomes packaged as a human baby: compacted down into bodily form—apparently "normal" on the outside.

I marvel at the fact that the Creator of it all should ever become one, genuine, "unearthly child." This Time-and-Space Lord who "upholds the universe by the word of His power"[26] and who controls the destiny of it all—this Lord becomes sustained by a human mother, dependent upon part of his own creation. The infinite, sovereign, outside-and-inside-of-Time God becomes shut into a finite, time-limited human form—the mystery which we call incarnation summed up in an amazingly forward-looking medieval prayer:

Welcome all wonders in one sight!
Eternity shut in a span.
Summer in winter, day in night,
heaven in earth and God in man.
Great little one whose all-embracing birth
brings earth to heaven, stoops heaven to earth.[27]

TARDIS—THE ACRONYM

Acronyms can be helpful in aiding our understanding of the nature and *modus operandi* of things, for example, the laser. How many people in the street know what the word *laser* stands for? Most recognize it as a device that generates a powerful, narrow beam of light. To tell them what L A S E R stands for, and to unpack the words represented by the acronym enables the eyes of some to be opened (and of many others to be glazed over—blinded not by the laser but by science!)[28][29]

When it comes to the TARDIS, we find the acronym defined in that very first episode by the Doctor's granddaughter: Time and Relative Dimension In

Space.[30][31] In today's world of wonder at both the size and intricate detail of our universe it's a very contemporary and relevant acronym some fifty years on. There are many current documentaries on popular science that follow scientists of celebrity status like Stephen Hawking[32] and UK TV's Brian Cox,[33] both eminent professors in their fields, presenting the scientific metaphors to describe the nature of the universe in which we live. It is very timely to take up their talk about the nature of creation which denies reference to any form of Creator. By using the metaphors presented to us in the fundamentals of *Doctor Who*, we may direct the masses to the reality of God underpinning the metaphors of science in a way that helps people see the Church not as an irrelevant institution or bunch of blinkered stalwarts, but as an engaging community of believers who make the Good News ever relevant to a new generation.

TARDIS AS ENGAGEMENT WITH A BIBLICAL UNDERSTANDING OF TIME AND SPACE

There is much to credit the so-called "classical model"[34] as it declares God's sovereignty, eternity, and power over all things. Its problems came, when faced with the rise of modern science, that it did not look for ways in which to integrate them, but rather retreated into a "God of the Gaps" mentality.[35] There are also parts of the Thomist[36] branch of the model that state that God is unperturbed by the world. Although it affirms the doctrines of predestination and God's universal omniscience, it struggles with these in the light of Einstein's discovery of relativity and all that that entails concerning the nature of time, and specifically that information transfer cannot exceed the velocity of light.[37] However, recent developments in cosmology come to the aid of the classical model and do away with the need for primary and secondary causes for God to act.[38] This latter thought is complex, yet dealt with very well by the TARDIS communicating with Clara through the burnt image on her hand in *Journey*, ultimately leading the Doctor to reset Time for them by reaching through a time rift in the TARDIS. He thus alters their history by removing the cause that afflicted them, out of the very situation arising from the original affliction!

Many people still live with that classical concept of time and the arrow of time: that time is uni-directional and relentless. Episodes like *Journey* help to challenge that view. Not surprisingly, those holding to a classical view have problems squaring God's sovereignty and foreknowledge with free will. To help them see that God can be both beyond our time and still active, I would lead them to consider a hypothetical world of intelligent creatures living in a three-dimensional world of x-y-t: *i.e.* they exist on a flat space of no depth, like the surface of a page in a book (please use your imagination!) These creatures are unaware of, and struggle to conceive of any z dimension, although they may express it mathematically. They are thus unaware of other "pages." As four-dimensional beings living in x-y-z-t, we can look at their existence, see their limitations and encompass them. We can intervene in their world by the fact we can move in and out of it, write on their 2D page with our 3D pencil, cross their boundaries because we can, and even create whole new "pages" of which they can never be aware. This intervention may delight or frighten them, or they may discredit it as an artifact of some scientific hypothesis contrived by their professors.

Now let us take this world and "upgrade" the metaphor by one dimension and translate it to refer to our relationship with God. We "live and move and have our being"[39] in x-y-z-t. We are unaware of, and struggle to conceive of another dimension, although we may express it mathematically. God, existing in five (or more) dimensions can look at our existence, see our limitations and encompass us—He can intervene in our world by the fact that he can move in and out of it in space-time with His own being. He can even create whole new universes of which we can never be aware.[40] This intervention may delight or frighten us, or we may discredit it as an artifact of some scientific hypothesis contrived by our professors.

The TARDIS helps us visualize such "rifts" in time and space. It is, after all, a machine that does *time* and *relative dimension* stuff. Moreover, such other dimensions are consistent with modern M-theory of multi-dimensional space,[41] with all but x-y-z-t "rolled up" so we do not perceive them. We must be careful that we do not say God is relegated *only* to the other dimensions for this would risk us again falling foul of a modern "God of the gaps" mentality.[42] But M-theory is *consistent* with postulating a mechanism for God "hearing" and answering prayer as represented by the physical state of our brains, and even answering them retrospectively, provided the timeline is left unaffected, as it finally was in *Journey*.

With God both intervening in and encompassing our time, He is present at the time of our intercessions, actions, decisions which we make freely, but is also "above" time so that He can see, in his concept of "now," what the outcome of that freely made decision will have been. He also intervenes by His Spirit to effect outcomes as part of the natural development of the world or even super-naturally. Following this thought development, several other theological conundrums become more understandable, such as God's omniscience and predestination.[43]

Thinking about the TARDIS as we think about God gives us a new way of visualizing these apparent conundrums for Whovians. Even those who are not can still sit through an episode with us and have their minds stretched to start thinking in the "inside-and-outside-of-time" way of God's working. "With God all things are possible"[44] and He can easily hold in tension what we may still think of as temporal distortions, much as the TARDIS tries to do. However, we must beware stretching the TARDIS metaphor too far because it has limitations that God does not. Take for example when the Doctor tries to rescue Rory from the weeping angels who have taken him to 1930's Manhattan. The TARDIS has difficulty landing because of the significant temporal distortions around the place where so many others have been imprisoned.[45] Also, it cannot resolve the older and younger Amy in one place in *The Girl who Waited*.[46] Even so, the TARDIS helps us to think outside of the limitations of our four dimensions to see how God works in and with Time.

THE TARDIS CONSOLE ROOM

Unlike the deck of Star Trek's *Enterprise* or *Voyager*, the TARDIS deck has always been hexagonal, set in the centre of the entrance room. There are some things that never seem to change. It may be dressed up differently to reflect the personality of each regeneration of the Doctor, but the essential control console is a hexagon with a dematerialization unit at the centre. Similarly we are reminded that, however we present him to a new generation, "Jesus Christ is the same yesterday and today and forever."[47]

While the engine room is at the centre and heart of the TARDIS, driving her every venture, the console room is the interface at which the Doctor and his traveling companions engage with the TARDIS and communicate with her. It is also the point of entry into the rest of the world. It's the place where all newcomers are amazed and say the inevitable about the relative sizes.

It may be stretching the metaphor a little, but we can think of this as the first point of contact with God for the new believer. As the doors of invitation are opened by one who already knows and understands the TARDIS, so a believer can open the doors to an outsider who, at the right time, can come to marvel at the wonders of God's salvation for themselves, to communicate with God through Christ, and to become ever a part of the long history of believers just as the TARDIS travelers through the past never really become separated from her. They may hesitate at first, like Clara who dismissed the Doctor's first invitation to come into what she refers to as his "snogging booth," or later on, "snog box"![48] But once inside this place of adventure, yet also a place of safety, travelers are always the ones who can say, "That which ... we looked upon and have touched with our hands ... we proclaim also to you, so that you too may have fellowship with us."[49] Once they move back to their original time and space, they may be "absent in body," but "with you in spirit."[50]

There is always that sense of safety yet adventure with God as there is in the TARDIS. The Doctor asks Clara, "Do you feel safe?" "Of course", she replies ... "I need to know if you feel safe ... you're not afraid of the future? ... anything could happen" ... "that's what I'm counting on!"[51]

TARDIS LIBRARY

There is a whole lot of stuff that the Doctor refers to on a regular basis in the generic format, "I remember how when we were on planet P at the time T in galaxy G, that's when I found... and learned about...". It's a wonderful thought that all of that is written down and stored in a special place in the TARDIS: a full history of what has been and will be in the lives of trillions of people and civilizations across the universes.

What I love about this room is that it gives us an image of the Scriptures in which we find and learn about God's character, our own salvation history in the outworkings of our own time, and what will be the eternal destiny for those who believe. Look at all those doors and corridors in *Journey* that Clara *doesn't* enter, like the astronomical telescope or swimming pool, not to mention the ones she passes, unopened. There is always more to discover in the riches of scripture about God and our bonding with Him.

Bringing these thoughts together I again think "Our God is too small." The Scriptures tell us about the *human* relationship with Him. They are not designed to tell us about an *alien's* relationship with God, should such aliens exist. From a scientific viewpoint I really can't see why other sentient species should not exist across the universe in forms we cannot even envisage.[52]

Stored within the heart of God, as stored within the TARDIS, is a love for *all* his creation. So with an eye to the TARDIS, when I read verses such as, "I have other sheep that are not of this fold. I must bring them also... so there will be one flock, one shepherd"[53] and, "while we were still weak, at the right time Christ died for the ungodly"[54] I read them with a mind-bogglingly new thought: God has a destiny for *all that are made in his image*. And any "other sheep" "out there" that are created with a free will that can disobey and fall out with God can be saved too. Not only so, but the Cross and all its implications for us, was (or will be) at the "right time" for them, too. Maybe even the "right time" could indicate that, in some way, the crucifixion and atonement were or will be somehow "simultaneous" across the bounds of the universe(s) so that for all sentient beings across all times and dimensions, it was also the "right time!" It would be lovely to think that their version of the Scriptures will also contain that verse. God is suddenly a whole lot bigger!

The TARDIS, like God, is gradually revealed in more and more detail as time passes, and each Doctor and the travelers within her come to understand her better. There are things the Doctor doesn't know about her, which slip out from time to time like, "the code is still a secret"[55] at the very start of the adventure, to, "this ship is infinite."[56]

PERSONALITY AND RELATIONSHIP WITH THE TARDIS

As I grew older and more discerning, I became aware of the growing relationship between the Doctor and the (mostly) human (and usually female) individuals who end up as his companion(s). I no longer just watched for the "techie" bits, getting bored with the more intimate and human scenes, but saw something more going on at a higher level. More recently we see the Doctor's relationship with the TARDIS herself, who can be a jealous personality![57] Even in earlier seasons we discover, "She's very temperamental when she's roused"[58] for example.

Ultimately we see her materialize into a humanoid form in *The Doctor's Wife* where the living consciousness of the TARDIS is locked in a humanoid body which enables the Doctor finally to converse with her. Needing a Time Lord to see the world, she says she selected the Doctor back on Gallifrey because he was "the only one mad enough" for such an odyssey.[59] The Doctor also depends on the TARDIS, from the simultaneous translation circuit to the fact that she can call him back from "nowhere."[60]

It takes time for others to get to know her, often from an "unbelieving" start as we see from Clara's dismissive, "you're not getting me to talk to your ship!" to which the Doctor replies, "it's important to me you get along."[61] In fact there is a tendency to move from talking of TARDIS as "it" to talking of TARDIS as "she."

Some, likewise, have a very academic view of God, and regard Him as impersonal. But we see this changing, too. There has been a great change in recent decades of no longer referring to the Holy Spirit as "it" but as "he." Just as the personal side of the TARDIS is discovered as the series develop so our relationship with Trinity does. Some of us have that genuine "epiphany" when we experience God in such a personal way and we react very emotionally as does the Doctor when encountering the "incarnate" TARDIS in *Wife*. But even those who do not have such a life-changing experience are still encouraged to engage with God in a personal way, from the heart and not just from the head.

Such relationship development is seen in the long-term as we witness Israel's initial fear of Yahweh, appeasing an essentially unknown deity mediated through prophets, through to growing as Christians with Jesus leading us to intimacy with God through his Spirit as Jesus prays for us, "that they may all be one, just as you, Father, are in me, and I in you, that they also may be in us, so that the world may believe that you have sent me."[62]

TARDIS AS SELF-REVELATION: OSSIFIED CREATURES

Clara discovers that the ossified creatures chasing her are actually made of her very own past and future. They are an ugly sight! She is not safe from them until she can, in the fullness of time, become properly acquainted with the

TARDIS. Likewise, we are not safe from our own past until we are redeemed by God and find our peace in Him. "The wages of sin is death."[63] and these ossified creatures are a scary and horrific reminder of this.

ENGINE ROOM

Ultimately, in *Journey* we discover, amazingly, that the heart of the TARDIS reflects the very heart of God and his love for his creation. We find that the TARDIS has, herself, contained the explosion of the engine room in order to preserve her occupants. She wishes to preserve them at all costs. It's a great reminder of the fact that God has withheld His judgment of us because of the Cross. All humanity stands condemned already, because of their unbelief.[64] But just as the TARDIS has withheld the devastating destruction in time, to save its travelers, so God has held off that "end of time destruction" to give us the opportunity to repent and believe, that we may be saved. The temporal rift provided by the TARDIS through which the Doctor reaches to redeem the situation is like the Cross by which the relationship of Trinity, one with another, is momentarily rifted as Jesus is forsaken[65] to redeem us from the inevitable destruction that otherwise awaits.

CONCLUSION

While we could go on to explore the Eye of Harmony, the Architectural Reconfiguration System, or the Room of Fire, that's for you, the reader to do. Like the intricacies of the faith, the TARDIS is vast; this is only the beginning. Studying something as surprising—yet constant—as this blue police box may lead us one step further: to consider "what is the breadth and length and height and depth, and to know the love of Christ that surpasses knowledge, that you may be filled with all the fullness of God."[66]

ENDNOTES

1 "The Snowmen." (Clara's answer is a first: "It's smaller on the outside.")
2 Romans 11:33.
3 Rom 10:1.
4 Following Paul's example. 1 Cor 9:22b, Acts 17:23 ff. The latter is Paul's classic address to the Athenian Areopagus, starting from their familiar ways to lead into the gospel.
5 Looking beyond *Doctor Who* for a moment, there are many, many metaphors with cult TV series and movies that we can take to engage their devotees. I also love *Star Trek, Star Wars*, the *Matrix, Men in Black*—some more seriously than others!
6 I started my study of science at John Ruskin Grammar School, Croydon, then at Cambridge University, where I also came to faith (1975). I began a career in microelectronics with what was then GEC (not GE!) and began to train as a lay minister in the Anglican Church. I moved into computer technology, quality control, documentation, and then IT training and technical authoring before becoming self-employed. In 2002 I was then dramatically called out of all

that and began training for the ministry at Trinity College, Bristol in 2004. I served a curacy in Colchester and currently serve as Priest in Charge in a parish near Haslemere, Surrey.

7   John 3:16—the Greek *kosmo* is the underlying text we usually translate as "world"—God's salvation perspective is bigger than you may think! Compare to 1 Cor 8:19-21 for God's liberation of creation. Remember the title of the classic book by John Bertram Phillips, *Your God is Too Small.*

8   Ian G. Barbour, Religion and Science, (London: SCM, 1998), 77.

9   Barbour 1998, 78-82. Sagan, Crick, Monod, and the Neo-Darwinist Dennett are prime examples. Bad science can also result from deeply held personal opinions, such as Einstein's "cosmological constant" (Schaeffer 2004, 2).

10 Barbour 1998, 82-84. The Catholic Church's reaction to Galileo, and modern-day Southern Baptists' view of evolution are prime examples.

11 Polkinghorne, John. 1996. *Searching for Truth.* Oxford: BRF, 40. Morris is one such protagonist of biblical fundamentalism and president of the Institute for Creation Research, San Diego, California in 1988. He strongly refutes evolution and supports all his ideas from direct quotations from the AV (e.g. Morris, Henry M. 1988. *Science and the Bible.* Amersham: Scripture Press, 35-42.)

12 Barbour, Religion and Science, 84-90.

13 Barbour, Religion and Science, 90-98.

14 Barbour 1998, 101. Arthur Peacocke is a biochemist and theologian who is willing to engage with both and "discusses at length how chance and law work together in cosmology, quantum physics, non-equilibrium thermodynamics, and biological evolution."

15 Barbour, Religion and Science, 104.

16 Ibid., 115-124.

17 There are several distinct models of Christ's atonement supported by scripture, all drawing metaphors from places like the market, the law courts, military victory: all helpful for a particular context yet none complete on its own.

18 The key to the Doctor's TARDIS took several forms over the years. Initially it resembled a plain key for a Yale lock, such as might be used with a genuine police box. During his third regeneration, the Doctor began experimenting with new designs for his key, coming up with several designs before settling on a spade-shaped silver key. The Fourth Doctor made even more radical designs, before eventually going back to the spade and Yale styles. The Yale key was used by the Fifth and Sixth Doctors while the Seventh had a fan-shaped key bearing the Seal of Rassilon. At some point, the Eighth Doctor returned to using the Yale key and the following Doctors have continued with that style.

19 Douglas Adams, Hitchhiker's Guide to the Galaxy (New York: Del Rey, 1995). Incidentally, the answer to the question is, according to the Guide, 42. To discover why, you will have to listen to this unique radio cult genre of Sci-Fi humor!

20 "but it was just a telephone box. . . a Police telephone box: I walked all round it. . . I walked all round it!" Ian. "An Unearthly Child."

21 "Journey to the Centre of the TARDIS."

22 OK, so it's not "real fact" kind of fact, but for the Whovian it's as-good-as when it comes to weighing up life against their Whovian universal view!

23 Acts 17:28 from Paul's Athenian address cited in footnote 4.

24 1 Cor 13:12.

25 Heb 1:2.

26 Heb 1:3.

27 Crashaw, Richard. 1612-1649. Full chorus, verse 1, in *In the Holy Nativity of our Lord.* Accessed 26/8/2014 http://www.poemhunter.com/poem/in-the-holy-nativity-of-our-lord/

28 It stands for Light Amplification by Stimulated Emission of Radiation. Generally, light is *"radiated"* by electrons "dropping" to a lower "orbit" round their atoms after they have been "pumped up" higher by heat or electricity. If you make a system of mirrors so that one ray of light goes up and down *"stimulating"* all the other pumped up atoms to *"emit"* light all at the same time, you

get huge "*amplification*" of *light* intensity. It's a bit like pumping up lots of balloons and firing an arrow through them all at once. You get a bigger bang!

29   Maybe there's another metaphor there in Jesus' own use of parables for seeing/blinding—cf. Mt 13:10-15, Mk 4:30, 33-34.

30   "An Unearthly Child."

31   Some dispute whether it should be TARDIS or Tardis—I think the latter, as we currently use Laser not LASER. And the word laser began to reach the ears of the public around the same time as TARDIS! But, as you will see throughout this book, my side in the dispute lost.

32   Stephen William Hawking CH CBE FRS FRSA (b. 1942) is an English theoretical physicist, cosmologist, author and Director of Research at the Centre for Theoretical Cosmology within the University of Cambridge. Among his significant scientific works have been gravitational singularity theorems in the framework of general relativity, and the theoretical prediction that black holes emit radiation. Hawking was the first to set forth a cosmology explained by a union of the general theory of relativity and quantum mechanics. He achieved success with works of popular science in which he discusses his own theories and cosmology in general such as his "A Brief History of Time." Hawking has a motor neurone disease that has progressed over the years. He is now almost entirely paralyzed and communicates through a speech generating device. He married twice and has three children.

33   Brian Edward Cox OBE (b. 1968) is an English physicist and former musician, Professor, a Royal Society University Research Fellow, PPARC Advanced Fellow at the University of Manchester. He is a member of the High Energy Physics group at the University of Manchester, and works on the ATLAS experiment at the Large Hadron Collider at CERN, near Geneva, Switzerland. Cox is best known to the public as the presenter of a number of science programmes for the BBC, boosting the popularity of subjects such as astronomy and physics. He also had some fame in the 1990s as the keyboard player for the pop band D:Ream.

34   Barbour, Religion and Science, 306-312.

35   This is no doubt partly due to the Classical Greek influence to think deeply but not to engage with observation. Polkinghorne 1996, 10.

36   Thomas Aquinas' world view, based on Greek Philosophy.

37   David Wilkinson, God, Time, and Stephen Hawking (Mill Hill, London: Monarch, 2001), 119.

38   Also note that the "Bell effect" implies that change to a particle which is one part of a quantum system will change another particle in that system simultaneously even though they are large distances apart (Lucas 1996, 38; 43-44).

39   Acts 17:28 again.

40   This language is consistent with "by Him all things were created, in heaven and on earth, visible and invisible … he is before all things, and in Him all things hold together." Col 1:16-17 .

41   Hawking, Stephen W. 1996. *A Brief History of Time*. Illustrated Edition; London: Bantam Press/ Transworld Publishers, 54.

42   Hawking 1996, 62. Hawking points out that the Catholic Church (and, I believe, many others) supported the Big Bang theory of 1951 as in accordance with the Bible. The risk is that if science then tends towards an oscillatory universe, or an inflationary one, there may be some serious theological back-tracking to do!

43   These follow on because they are all time-related issues. Omniscience requires information traveling faster that light: but this is a limitation only on our 4D universe. Predestination requires God's knowledge of the outcome of a free choice made earlier in our time-frame, which in our hypothesis, *can* be known to God "before." Hawking explores at length the possibilities of knowing the future, time travel and the like but it is always from our point of view, from within the four dimensions by which we are bounded (Hawking 2001, 101 ff).

44   Mt 19:26.

45   "The Angels Take Manhattan."

46   "The Girl Who Waited."

47   Heb 13:8.

48   "The Bells of Saint John."
49   1 Jn 1:1-4.
50   Col 2:5.
51   "Journey."
52   The Daleks are one such example and I believe one of the scary things about them as a child is that they are *not* humanoid! Occasionally, *Doctor Who* and *Star Trek* do push out our thinking beyond the inevitable humanoid forms.
53   Jn 10:16.
54   Romans 5:6.
55   The Doctor, "An Unearthly Child."
56   The Doctor, "Journey."
57   *Journey* and *Clara and the TARDIS* "Searching for the Lost Bedroom." Doctor Who, mini episode, Series 7 DVD.
58   The Doctor (3), *"The Time Monster,"* season 9, episode 4. Other notable quotes are, "don't touch a thing. The TARDIS will get huffy if you mess." *"Journey,"* minute 12, and, "I can feel a TARDIS tantrum coming on," minute 15.
59   "The Doctor's Wife."
60   The "extreme emergency" knob that Jo Grant engages to get the Doctor (3) to rematerialize when he's lost "out there, somewhere." *"The Time Monster,"* episode 5.
61   "Journey."
62   Jn 17:21.
63   Rom 6:23.
64   Jn 3:16-18.
65   Mt 27:46.
66   Eph 3:18-19.

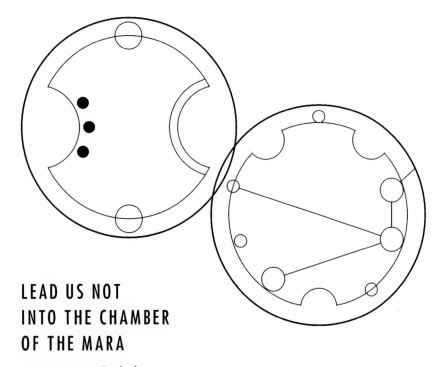

LEAD US NOT
INTO THE CHAMBER
OF THE MARA

TEMPTATION: *Snakedance*
ORIGINAL AIRDATE: JANUARY 18, 1983

My first introduction to *Doctor Who* was walking through my friend Elspeth's living room and glimpsing Matt Smith's face on the television. After that, I remember hearing something about two hearts, Daleks, and listening to friends argue over who was better—Tennant or Smith.[1] I eventually gave in, watched the first two seasons, and cried when Rose left . . . refusing to ever watch *Doctor Who* again. Of course that didn't last very long. In a span of eight months, I had watched 27 seasons, and for a birthday present this year I received a sonic screwdriver.

The thing about *Doctor Who* that makes it so irresistible (and nearly above critique) is that it is always changing. If you do not like a particular episode, there are well over eight hundred other ones to try. There are different Doctors, Companions, locations, and enemies.[2] I think that this is what has made the series so addicting over the past half century, and why I couldn't stop watching, even when Rose got stuck in a parallel universe. In fact, it was so addicting that I felt compelled to get my father hooked, too.

When I first introduced *Doctor Who* to my father, I had a lot of explaining to do. I did not want to show him the first episode I had watched, so there was a great deal of "The rest of the Time Lords are extinct..." and "Yes, that is because of the Daleks..." and "There was a Time War..." and "Well, it's *sonic*...." I had to explain the Weeping Angels and Regenerations at least three times before either concept stuck. And, of course, the TARDIS—well, you can imagine how that went. My father is a well-read teacher of the Great Books,[3] so I suspect that the lengthy explanations were due to the fact that he wasn't really paying attention most of the time. But one of the early clarifying questions he asked me was if *Doctor Who* had any Christian themes. My immediate response was "Of course not—it isn't made by Christians. It is totally non-religious Sci-Fi." My father had taught me that every good story is infused with Christian themes, but I was sure that this couldn't apply to *Doctor Who*.

A few months after I finished watching the new seasons, I bravely ventured into the classic *Doctor Who* episodes. Twenty-six seasons seemed a bit daunting—some were even in black and white. But it was *Doctor Who*, so—like Matt Smith in his first episode[4]—I jumped in. Geronimo! Soon, I was addicted. Despite my doubts, the old episodes offered the same amusing qualities that I loved in the current run of the show.

Eventually, I reached the episode *Snakedance,* featuring Peter Davidson[5] as the Doctor. The themes in this episode reminded me so much of the concept of temptation that I started to have second thoughts about my quick dismissal of my father's initial question. Maybe the series *did* have Christian themes. After all, every good story has a Christian theme of some sort—and *Doctor Who* is a very good story. The first episode of this serial aired on January 18, 1983, and it was written by Christopher Bailey. It includes the Fifth Doctor, along with his Companions Tegan and Nyssa, and features the return of the Mara.[6] Tegan Jovanka was an Australian air stewardess trainee (she wandered into the Fourth Doctor's TARDIS when she mistook it for a genuine police box) and Nyssa was a native of the planet Traken.[7]

In this episode the enemy, The Mara, is an alien from an earlier episode who is known for possessing the minds of other people. When the Doctor's Companion, Tegan, starts having odd dreams about a cave, and is very troubled, the Doctor seeks after the cave to find out what's going on. In the town where the cave lies, Tegan is taken over by the Mara and runs away from the doctor, wrecking havoc in the city. She comes across a deceptive gypsy who lies to people through fortune-telling; an arrogant, rich man, Lon, who is line for the throne; and a greedy con man, Dugdale, who is desperate for money. The Mara, through Tegan, tricks and possesses both Lon and Dugdale, trying to find a precious stone that will help her take over the city. The Doctor and Nyssa, meanwhile, are in the royal jail, and upon escaping, seek after Tegan to try and release her from The Mara.

The episode begins with the Doctor trying to lead them down a path to an ultimate goal, the cave, where all their burdens (the Mara) will be released. Much like God tries to lead us down a path to a place where our burdens can be released. However, just like us, Tegan, controlled by her burden, strays from the path. One of the first things that happens after Tegan runs away is that she finds herself in the hands of a gypsy. She is shown a vision and has a panic attack. The whole village surrounds her tent wondering what could frighten someone so much. Sin harms not only you, but those around you. Tegan's possessive side has not only hurt her, but is hurting others as well. This is also shown in Lon, who is a nasty person, and is eventually tempted and possessed by the Mara.

A realistic aspect of this process is the development of the sin. Tegan, Lon, and the gypsy all start out doing simple, seemingly insignificant things: disrespecting others, deceiving strangers, and throughout the episode, the temptation grows like bacteria until they are manipulating and harming others. Sin is not a one-time thing. It's not something you give into once, and then slip back into sinlessness. Not only does it cease to leave, but it grows into something much worse—every second—as you give in more and more.

When I think about temptation, I'm immediately reminded of King David. The song *Hallelujah*[8] says of David, "His faith was strong but you needed proof, he saw her bathing on the roof her beauty in the moonlight, overthrew you . . ." I love those lyrics because they acknowledge that in spite of his sin, David's faith was strong. Some people assume that only the weak are tempted, that only the weak give in to temptation. But everyone is tempted, and everyone gives in. Temptation isn't our fault, but we are responsible for our reactions to temptation. The key goal when faced with temptation is to resist sin and walk in obedience. King David did not resist sin and he did not walk in obedience, nor do we in our everyday lives. David is tempted to lust after a woman, and is led to deception, murder, and dishonor. If we deny God so easily, what is to stop us from doing the same? What is to stop the Maras of this world from corrupting us? What is to stop the Lons of this world from being corrupted?

Jesus was tempted three times in the wilderness. First, Satan tempted Him by telling Him to turn the rocks into bread, for Jesus was hungry. Then, Satan asks Him to prove His great power by jumping from the Temple and having the angels save him. Third, Satan promises all the kingdoms of the world if Jesus bow down and worship him. But to this; all of these promises and proposals; our great Lord denies His enemy. We are told repeatedly that Jesus is without sin, that He is perfect in every way. But we are quick to dismiss the temptation Jesus must have felt standing with Satan that day, the sharp hunger in His stomach, the ability but refusal to shove His power in Satan's face, the images of the streets filling up with His worshipers and subjects after He had been denied by so many people. I know I would have kissed the ground Satan walked on, bowed on my face if I was promised one kingdom, much less the entire world. For David, the mere ability to have Bathsheba to himself was enough to slaughter an honest man. For Dugdale, the idea of a sack of gold was enough to steal what was not his. But Jesus, our humble and perfect King, the righteous servant of God, denies Satan, resists sin, and walks in obedience.

It is interesting to compare Jesus' temptations to those in *Snakedance*. Both Dugdale and Jesus are tempted with physical aspects, Jesus with bread, and Dugdale with riches. Both Lon and Jesus are tempted with mental aspects, power and respect. Both the gypsy and Jesus are tempted with spiritual aspects, fortune-telling and worship. Even though this episode is about an alien who possesses people, the same principles apply to temptation. The people in this episode who followed directions and trusted the Doctor were not conquered by evil. In the same way, when we follow Jesus and trust His Word, we can overcome evil. But those who were fickle, weak, and tempted, fell at evil's feet.

In *Snakedance*, the Doctor agrees to allow himself to be bitten by the snake to have his mind opened, so he could conquer the Mara. This is the ultimate Christ-like act. The Doctor knows that he has little time to save his friend, and the people of the city. But even so, he puts himself at risk. My first reaction was thinking that I would never, *ever* let myself be bitten by a snake for someone— the Doctor was a real hero. Then I thought about what Jesus had to go through, and the Doctor looks rather small in comparison.

Being tempted isn't a sign of weakness. Jesus was tempted. By denying temptation, you are showing Satan that you are God's property, and that he can't do anything to you. You are showing your trust in God and your defiance in the face of sin; you are showing your belief that God can and did save you, and nothing will ever change that. You are showing that you know that you will one day see him, and reach ultimate maturity and perfection. But by accepting temptation, you are showing Satan that you are free ground, and that you are weak. You have declared your distrust in Jesus, you have strayed from obedience, and you have accepted death. Once you have done so, you can only become alive again through confession and faith in Christ. We belong to God. We are His masterpieces. We are Satan's Most Wanted, and God's most beloved. God will stop at nothing to rescue his lost lambs, but we cannot help but to become lost all over again. We are stiff necked and gullible. We are ungrateful and untrustworthy. But we are loved. We are loved, and we have been promised a world free of the Mara, temptations and sins, a world of infinite communion with God, and we must not forget that promise. We should learn from people like David, we should feel a shimmering hope from Jesus. Just as the Mara manipulates and deceives Tegan, Satan manipulates and deceives us. We must guard our hearts from Satan and focus our minds on God.

When I started *Doctor Who,* I didn't expect to have a theological breakthrough. However, I think there is a very powerful theme behind this seemingly insignificant serial. There will come times when we look into the eyes of temptation and we, our hearts and minds solely and firmly fixed on God, will walk away. We will walk right away without pain or worry or sin, because Satan has no control over us. But, in our lives, there will be times when we flee from protection, we will desert God and his guidance and we won't give it a second thought. And, later on, when we look down at ourselves in confusion and disgust, we will wonder why we left our home. Then, as we crawl back in shame and agony, our forgiving Father will embrace us and welcome us home. He will tell us with utter jubilance and happiness that He, our all powerful and kind God, has conquered the Mara and has banished the wicked, and we will rejoice. We will rejoice because our burdens will have been released.

ENDOTES

1   Totally Tennant.
2   Although, truthfully, the Cybermen *do* show up quite often. If you don't like them, you may find enjoying the series a bit of a challenge.
3   That is, books that are classic works in the canon of Western culture like Shakespeare, Churchill, Dickens, and other writers that the Doctor has visited.
4   The Eleventh Hour
5   Tennant's father-in-law. Davison's daughter from his second marriage is actress Georgia Moffett. She played the Doctor's daughter Jenny in the episode "The Doctor's Daughter". So in a way, she is the daughter of two Doctors. It's all rather timey-whimey.
6   A villain who the Doctor had battled in an earlier episode, *Kinda.*
7   A planet in the system Mettula Orionsis and homeworld of the Trakenites, a race of pacifists. It was said that there was so much good in the air on Traken that evil would just shrivel up and die.
8   "Hallelujah" by Canadian singer-songwriter Leonard Cohen was originally released on his album *Various Positions* (1984).

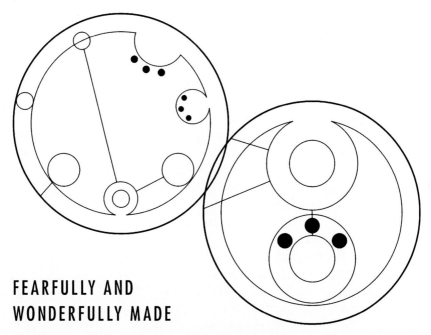

FEARFULLY AND
WONDERFULLY MADE

SANCTITY OF LIFE: *The Rebel Flesh/The Almost People* and *Kill the Moon*
ORIGINAL AIRDATES: MAY 21/28 2011 AND OCTOBER 4, 2014

In *The Fellowship of the Ring,* when Frodo is discussing the history of the Ring with Gandalf, Frodo says that he cannot feel any pity for the miserable creature Gollum, and that Gollum deserves death. Gandalf's reply was almost as shocking to my child self as it was to Frodo:

"Deserves it! I daresay he does. Many that live deserve death. And some that die deserve life. Can you give it to them? Then do not be too eager to deal out death in judgment. For even the very wise cannot see all ends."[1]

When I discovered *Doctor Who* years later, the Doctor reminded me of a more whimsical, irresponsible Gandalf.[2] Both serve as guides to Companions on adventures, both are wise, witty scholars; they are both nearly immortal, and they both value life. Like Gandalf, the Doctor is hesitant to take life, or dole out judgment. Instead, he seeks to preserve even the life of his enemies in the hope that they might experience a change of heart.[3]

Though the Doctor and Gandalf are fictional, their regard for life has a Biblical precedence. In Genesis 9 when God reestablishes His covenant with Noah and his descendants, God declares, "Whoever sheds the blood of man, by man shall his blood be shed, for God made man in his own image." [4] Outside of the government,[5] there is no institution, group, or single person Biblically authorized to deal out death, no matter how wise.

With the advent of reproductive technologies, socially acceptable abortion, and "right to die" legislation,[6] it has been the doctor (sometimes alongside the patient), and not the judge, handing out life and death sentences. This is not the function of a doctor, and it flies in the face of the thousands of years of medical practice since The Hippocratic Oath.[7]

A traditional doctor does not take lives, but fights to preserve them. In *Doctor Who*, we are reminded of this in the recent 50th anniversary special: "The Day of the Doctor." Companion Clara challenges the three Doctors on their decision to destroy Gallifrey, and the Eleventh Doctor maintains that there is no other way; he doesn't know what to do.

Clara tells him, "Be a doctor. You told me the name you chose was a promise. What was the promise?"[8]

The other two Doctors respond, "Never cruel or cowardly. Never give up, never give in."[9] Doctors save lives, they don't take them.

One of the most fascinating aspects of *Doctor Who* is that its hero is a doctor. When the show first aired in 1967, other popular television programs starred superheroes, secret agents, cowboys, adventurers, and detectives. Though eventually revealed to be a Time Lord, the Doctor is often simply identified as a doctor. From the Latin *docere*, meaning "to instruct or teach," the word later came to mean a physician or healer. Since *Doctor Who* originated as a science program for families, a time-traveling "Doctor" is the perfect protagonist.

Over its lengthy run, *Doctor Who* has explored ideas about space, anthropology, and time, gradually expanding its range to ethical dilemmas. From racial cleansing to genocide, life and death are examined through the Doctor's alien perspective. His role as teacher and healer, alongside his tendency to meddle puts him in the way of hard moral decisions that affect nations, planets, or the entire universe. More importantly, it puts him in situations where the value of individual lives must be considered.

Despite witnessing the brevity of human life, the Eleventh Doctor maintains that each life is significant, declaring, "In nine-hundred years of time and space, I've never met anyone who wasn't important."[10]

As Christians, we agree with the Doctor. Every person is created for and by God. According to the Scriptures, we bear the likeness and image of God:

> Then God said, "Let us make man in our image, after our likeness. And let them have dominion over the fish of the sea and over the birds of the heavens and over the livestock and over all the earth and over every creeping thing that creeps on the earth." So God created man in

his own image, in the image of God he created him; male and female he created them. And God blessed them. And God said to them, "Be fruitful and multiply and fill the earth and subdue it, and have dominion over the fish of the sea and over the birds of the heavens and over every living thing that moves on the earth."[11]

Though our natures have been warped and tainted by sin, we retain the image of God, somewhat like a ruined cathedral or temple retains the image of its former glory. As God's image bearers, we have value, and responsibilities. One of these responsibilities is the preservation of life and the punishment of those who disregard it.[12] We are unique, handcrafted creatures, "made in secret, intricately woven in the depths of the earth."[13] All arguments for the preservation and treatment of life must stand upon this foundation.

In the universe of *Doctor Who*, populated by monsters, aliens, and humans, most of humanity's value is due to its persistence and hope. Though the worth and the meaning of individual lives have been established many times in the series, they are closely examined in both the two-part episode "The Rebel Flesh" and "The Almost People," and the recent episode, "Kill the Moon." In the former, The Eleventh Doctor takes the side of the "almost human" Flesh, opposing his human Companions and the Flesh's human creators. In "Kill the Moon," the Twelfth Doctor abdicates almost completely, leaving his Companion Clara and two other women to make the ultimate moral decision. Both episodes openly question and examine the value of life, human and otherwise.

In "The Rebel Flesh" and "The Almost People," the Eleventh Doctor and Companions Amy and Rory encounter the Flesh, a programmable substance that can perfectly replicate humans. Their ideas of humanity are upended. By challenging our notions of personhood, this episode is an interesting look at the sanctity of life.

In "The Rebel Flesh," the Doctor and his Companions visit an acid factory in the Earth's future. This factory is run by workers with a unique way of avoiding workplace injuries: they have doppelgangers, or Gangers, who do all the deadly acid-mining for them. These Gangers are formed from the Flesh, a giant vat of bubbling goop able to take on the form and personality of its controller. The industrial workers control their Flesh avatars from full body machine systems. Safe in harnesses, the controllers use the "disposable" Flesh bodies to conduct their deadly work, never questioning the destruction of something that might have gained human consciousness.

The Flesh bodies look and act exactly like their human counterparts. As Cleaves, the factory supervisor, informs the Doctor, the degree of detail the Flesh is able to copy is amazing:

CLEAVES: Replicate a living organism down to the hairs on its chinny chin chin. Even clothes. And everything's identical. Eyes, voice . . .
DOCTOR: Mind, soul?
CLEAVES: Don't be fooled, Doctor. It acts like life but still needs to be controlled by us.
DOCTOR: You said it could grow. Only living things grow.[14]

Cleaves has talked herself into being comfortable with what she's doing. After all, it's for a good cause. The bodies are dispensable, unlike Cleaves herself. She is distances herself from the Flesh and its capabilities with clinical logic: "Moss grows. It's not more than that."[15] Her response is reminiscent of Dr. Michael J. Sandel's arguments supporting embryonic stem-cell research. His analogy is that acorns are to oak trees, what embryos are to adult humans. Sandel argues that though embryos have the potential for human life, they are no more human than an acorn is an oak tree.[16]

Like Sandel, Cleaves ignores the moral question of using the Flesh at all, and points to its convenience and lack of consciousness as valid reasons for continuing the practice. In her mind, the benefits outweigh any moral questions. "This acid is so dangerous; we were losing a worker every week. So now, we mine the acid using these doppelgangers. Or Gangers. If these bodies get burnt or fall in the acid . . ."[17]

Buzzer's Ganger finishes her sentence, "Then who the hell cares, right?"[18]

The other workers, Jennifer, Jimmy, and Dicken, agree with Cleaves and Buzzer. They see the Flesh's potential for life, but because it's logical and expedient for them to use the Gangers, they continue to ignore what is right in front of them. They are more concerned about their own personal peace and affluence than the morality of their job.

Though Flesh technology is fictional, the humans' reactions are plausible. It is an imitation of life. They have no reason to feel kinship to something that only looks like them. The Gangers are a sub-class of expendable tools, or so they tell themselves.

The Doctor isn't convinced about the Flesh's lack of consciousness, and he's also concerned for the factory workers. There's a solar storm about the factory, but the workers refuse to leave. Instead, they harness up and the Doctor gets to observe the Flesh forming an identical Jennifer. It looks exactly like her, but the real Jennifer controls it. Wide eyed, the Doctor observes, "Well, I can see why you keep it in a church. Miracle of life."[19]

The workers still try to write him off, "It's just gunge," Buzzer says.[20] They're ignoring the obvious, that any living organism with a mind and consciousness isn't just "gunge." Sadly, this point of view isn't science fiction at all.

Personhood has been a matter of debate in both political and moral arenas for decades, and especially since *Roe vs. Wade*. The point at which a baby begins to be a "baby" is still hotly debated. If a person is defined as a conscious being, productive in society and aware of their own existence, that automatically rules out infants, the severely disabled, and the mentally ill. Instead, as Gilbert Meilaender puts it, "Personhood is not something we "have" at some point . . . Rather, as embodied spirits or inspirited bodies, we are persons throughout the whole of that life. One whom we might baptize, one for who we might still pray, one for whom the Spirit of Christ may still intercede "with sighs too deep for words" (Rom. 8:26) – such a one cannot be for us less than a person."[21]

The implausibility of the Flesh aside, the Doctor is right to get the workers thinking. He is also intent on getting them out alive. Before he can disconnect the power systems, the whole factory is hit by the solar storm. A direct strike knocks the Doctor unconscious and hits the vat of Flesh. For anyone who has read Frankenstein, it is obvious where the Flesh is headed.[22]

When the Doctor wakes, the Gangers are nowhere in sight. Cleaves declares that the Gangers returned to pure Flesh as soon as the link (between worker and Ganger) was shut down; but she is mistaken. The Gangers were animated by the storm and they're seeking to connect to their lives, searching for confirmation that their transferred memories are real.

Cleaves and the other workers are appalled, but the Doctor points out that the Gangers' lives were bequeathed, not stolen. "You gave them this. You poured in your personalities, emotions, traits, memories, secrets, everything. You gave them your lives. Human lives are amazing. Are you surprised they walked off with them?"[23]

This suggests another troubling aspect of cloning. If everyone is created as unique individuals, how would cloning fit into the picture? Though the Flesh is impossible, the ethical questions it raises are valid. After all, our beliefs about cloning tie into our fundamental beliefs about life's value, inception, and meaning.

In 2008, a human embryo was reportedly cloned from adult stem cells.[24] Cloning embryos for the purpose of implantation and eventual birth is still illegal worldwide, as are most other forms of human cloning, so the embryo's only purpose would be research and development. These hypothetical clones would be, again, in the words of Gilbert Meilaender, "a class of embryos that it would be a crime *not* to destroy." [25] Humans, the great copiers, assume they can improve creation by imitating what God has already made. But, they don't usually think about the consequences of taking away that God-given uniqueness. If life, genes, and cells become commodities, the value of life will decrease exponentially.

If there are two copies of the same person, which one is real? This is the next problem in "The Rebel Flesh." With wandering Gangers and scared humans on his hands, it's up to the Doctor to keep the peace. He also has to convince the factory workers that the Gangers are alive, equally valid, and consider themselves to be exactly the same people they were cloned from. As the Doctor explains to Buzzer, "You both have the same childhood memories, just as clear, just as real." The Gangers are also scared, and "struggling to come to terms with an entire life in their heads."[26]

Though the monsters are the workers' own making (and identical to them in every way), the workers assume that the Gangers will destroy them. Of course, some of the workers turn out to be Gangers, convinced they are the originals. After Jennifer is revealed as a Ganger, her plea, "Just let us live!" becomes the overarching cry of the Gangers for the rest of the episodes. They can't understand why their lives are any less valuable than the people they copied.

Next, the Cleaves accompanying the Doctor is exposed as a Ganger, but she is so like the real Cleaves that she refuses to believe her own mind on the matter. She has unintentionally fooled the other workers, and proven the Doctor's point, but her revelation turns all but the Doctor against her. Like Jennifer, she claims, "We are living," before running away.

Living is very important to the Gangers. They state it as proof of their own validity. But what does it mean to be alive? Is it just a fully functioning nervous system, a brain that makes us alive, or a higher form of consciousness? According to Webster's Dictionary, life is "the quality that distinguishes a vital and functional being from a dead body," and "a principle or force that is considered to underlie the distinctive quality of animate beings."[27]

According to The Declaration of Independence, life is a basic right of *humanity*: "All men are created equal . . . endowed by their Creator with certain *unalienable Rights*," and "among these are Life, Liberty, and the pursuit of Happiness."[28] If you have picked up a newspaper, turned on the news, or listened to news radio lately, you've heard a lot about "rights." Whether the right to life, the right to choose, the right to marriage, or the right to remain silent, individual rights are central to most of the major disputes in the United States.

What sort of rights would a clone, a cloned embryo, or a normal embryo have? As they aren't technically defined as persons, under our current laws, they would have no rights at all. This is easier to assert on paper than if you could come face to face with one of these "non-persons."

This situation is exactly what happens to Rory Williams, one of the Doctor's Companions. He stumbles upon Jennifer/Ganger, who relates exact memories about her childhood and claims that she *is* Jennifer Lucas; she is not a factory part. When Rory asks where the real Jennifer is, the Ganger responds, "I am Jennifer Lucas. I remember everything that happened in her entire life.... I feel everything she has ever felt and more. I'm not a monster! I am me. Me! Me! Me! Why did they do this to us?"[29]

The Doctor continues in his quest to fix the situation, attempting to convince the others that the Gangers are not dangerous, but valid, living beings. "The Flesh was never merely moss. These are not copies. The storm has hardwired them. They are becoming people."[30]

The workers have trouble accepting this, but the Doctor continues in spite of them. "We were all jelly once. Little jelly eggs sitting in goop. We are not talking about an accident that needs to be mopped up. We are talking about sacred life. Do you understand?" The Doctor's use of language is intriguing. He is inferring that any potential sentient life, no matter what the form, should be treated as life. Embryos (as little jelly eggs in goop) are human beings at their earliest state of development, and no less human than a teenager or an infant.

In their argument for the full personhood status of an embryo, Robert P. George and Christopher Tollefsen write:

> When it is a matter of race or ethnicity, color or gender, origin or out-
> look, our culture resolutely and rightly holds that what matters is the fact
> of humanity, and not any other property shared by some but not others.
> But, by the same token, in considering the status of embryonic humans,
> what should matter is the fact of their humanity. They should not be re-
> garded as inferior to other members of the human family based on age,
> size, location, stage of development, or condition of dependency."[31]

There is nothing accidental about created life, and the Doctor is completely right in asserting so. Of course, their validity aside, the Gangers are still copies of real, actual people. They act and think alike. For example, both Jimmy and Jimmy/Ganger want to make it home for "his" son's birthday. Both have the same memories and feelings. The Doctor sums it up, "It's a right old mess," but he's still determined to get everyone out alive.

Human Cleaves has other plans, and she shows up armed with a circuit probe. The probe has enough to voltage to kill humans and Gangers, and Cleaves is ready to use it. Despite the Doctor's objections, Cleaves refuses to be persuaded. "Sorry. They're monsters. Mistakes. They have to be destroyed." When she proceeds to kill a Ganger, she calls it "decommissioned."

The observant viewer will notice the importance of language in these ep-isodes. While the Doctor (and the Gangers themselves) refers to the Gangers as "life, people, souls," Cleaves uses "monsters" and "mistakes." Monsters are dangerous, a threat to humanity. Mistakes are something you shrug off, maybe apologize for, and clean up.

Likewise, language is integral to debates about the sanctity of life. Even the phrase "sanctity of life" is a way of using language to influence the hearer. It is much harder to "kill" than to "end." It is barbaric to "kill a baby," but it sounds clinical to "terminate a pregnancy." In his discussion of how biotechnological advancements and modifications might affect our view of the human body, Leon R. Kass emphasizes how proper description and terminology are "crucial to moral evaluation." He continues:

One should try to call things by their right names. One should not encumber thought by adopting fuzzy concepts. And one should not try to solve the moral question by terminological sleight of hand—the way that some scientists today try to win support for cloning-for-biomedical-research—by denying that the cloning of embryos is cloning or that the initial product is an embryo. In this area especially the terminological question is crucial, but also hard. And, I confess at the start, although I have tried to find one, I have no simple solution: I see no clear way of speaking about this subject using simple, trouble-free distinctions.[32]

Note the kinds of words used in the famous passage from Psalm 139. The Psalmist describes human creation as personal. God forms each of us with a craftsman's care:

For you *formed* my inward parts; you *knitted* me together in my mother's womb. I praise you, for I am fearfully and wonderfully *made*. Wonderful are your works; my soul knows it very well. My frame was not hidden from you, when I was being made in secret, *intricately woven* in the depths of the earth. Your eyes saw my unformed substance; in your book were written, every one of them, the days that were formed for me, when as yet there was none of them.[33]

Returning to "The Rebel Flesh," although the Gangers are not human, they are very much alive. Cleaves distances herself from their lives because they are unnatural; the Gangers should have never been made. But killing them is equally, if not more, immoral.

Of course, the Doctor is the only one who seems to grasp the real gravity of the situation, "You stopped his heart. He had a heart. Aorta, valves, a real human heart. And you stopped it."

When Cleaves jumps from fearing the Flesh to destroying it, she is not just killing a lump of flesh, but a living organism that firmly believes it is human. It is also a being that she, as the supervisor, is personally responsible. This betrayal turns the Gangers against the humans for good. Like Frankenstein's monster, they are rejected by their creators and resort to violence.

Disregard for life goes hand in glove with disregard for the Creator of life. After all, an insult to the image of God is an insult to God. The Bible is very clear when it comes to murder. "You shall not murder (interpreted 'kill' in some translations)"[34] is one of the Ten Commandments. Murder was a crime punishable by death, a life for a life.[35]

Hypothetical clones, as humans once-removed, are the image of their creator, mankind, who are in turn, created in the image of God. The desecration of an image is an affront to the source of the image. John Davis writes, "Just as desecration of a nation's flag is an attack on the values of the nation that the flag represents, so an attack on the life of man is an attack on the majesty of God who created man to be His representative on earth."[36]

Though both the Gangers and the workers are out for blood, the Doctor and Rory are convinced they can still find a solution. Jennifer/Ganger also has a solution: destroy the humans and start a revolution. She doesn't understand why the Gangers should suffer for humans.

Again, inviting comparisons to the monster in *Frankenstein*, Jennifer/Ganger is furious with her maker and the entire human race. "They will melt you. Have you become so human that you've forgotten the truth? Don't you remember all the times you were decommissioned, or should I say, executed?" She has "declared everlasting war against the species."[37] Her steps in this war include imprisoning the humans, and killing several of them. In embracing her role as a monster, Jennifer/Ganger has lost any traces of humanity.

In the final act of "The Almost People," the Gangers and the humans must accept each other as people defined by their actions, not their nature. None of them had a choice in their creation, but they can choose how they respond. The survivors give their lives meaning by resisting revenge and rage, represented by Jennifer's Ganger, and head back into the world determined to change things for the better. The Doctor gave them purpose and hope, and reminded them of the value of life.

If this ending seems a bit tidy and trite, it is. *Doctor Who* is just a television show, and it can only serve as a metaphor. The Doctor, like all doctors, is not a god. In the words of Gilbert Meilaender, "Doctors are not saviors, and the best doctors know that, even if they only think of themselves as cooperating with the powers of nature... They are lordly and awesome in their technical prowess, but they are not the Lord whom death could not hold."[38]

Because he isn't a god or a perfect savior, the Doctor sometimes backs down from his stalwart protection of life. One of the most notable examples was in the recent episode, "Kill the Moon," which can be viewed as an abortion analogy.

In "Kill the Moon," the darker, grimmer Twelfth Doctor, his Companion Clara, and a stowaway from Clara's class, Courtney Woods, travel to the moon in 2049. They end up on a shuttle filled with nuclear bombs, crewed by the last astronauts. Humanity has lost all interest in space, and Captain Lundvik and her crew have only come because the moon's gravity has changed, causing massive natural disasters on earth.

Naturally, the Doctor asks Lundvik what she plans to do about it. She takes a case from the wall, and gives him a look, "That's what you do with aliens, isn't it? Blow them up?"[39]

After they establish that the moon is truly disintegrating, and lose both of Lundvik's astronaut's to the spider-like "germs," the Doctor finally discovers the truth.

"The moon isn't breaking apart. Well, actually, it is breaking apart, and rather quickly. We've got about an hour and a half. But that isn't the problem. It's not infested." The Doctor produces a scan, or rather, an ultrasound, that he took with his sonic screwdriver. The scan reveals a giant baby, albeit a dragonish, alien baby.

The Doctor finally explains his findings, "The moon isn't breaking apart. The moon is hatching . . . the moon's an egg."

He continues, "I think that it's unique. I think that's the only one of its kind in the universe. I think that that is utterly beautiful."

Their silent awe is interrupted by Lundvik. "How do we kill it?"

Clara is astonished. "Why'd you want to kill it?"

Courtney, innocent and young, states the obvious, "It's a little baby!"

What neither Clara nor Courtney realizes is that Lundvik doesn't *want* to kill anything. Lundvik thinks she only has one choice: let the creature live, or save humanity. Like Cleaves from "The Rebel Flesh," Lundvik is not cruel, she's a good person. However, she's pragmatic and terrified. Like Cleaves, Lundvik thinks that destroying the threat is the only way to guarantee the safety of the human race.

Violence is often the first recourse of someone who is afraid. It's much easier to destroy the problem, or run away from it, than to fix it. In the case of abortion, the problem is a pregnancy that is, for various reasons, unwanted. Violence, especially toward women and children, is symptomatic of cultural disease. Mother Teresa once denounced abortion as the "greatest destroyer of peace today," and continued,

"How do we persuade a woman not to have an abortion? As always, we must persuade her with love. The father of that child, whoever he is, must also give until it hurts. By abortion, the mother does not learn to love, but kills even her own child to solve her problems. And by abortion, the father is told that he does not have to take any responsibility at all for the child he has brought into the world. Any country that accepts abortion is not teaching the people to love, but to use any violence to get what they want."[40]

According to the Bible, "There is no fear in love, but perfect love casts out fear."[41] As humans snared by sin, we are often afraid. However, love and fear cannot dwell together. Likewise, love and selfishness are not compatible. Abortion, or the taking of one life for the convenience of another, is usually an act of fear or selfishness.

In "Kill the Moon," Lundvik is blinded by fear, so she continues to oppose both Clara and Courtney. For once, the Doctor refuses to have an overt opinion, "Kill the moon . . . If that's what you want to do . . . A hundred nuclear bombs set off right where we are, right on top of a living, vulnerable creature? It'll never feel the sun on its back."

Lundvik gets to the point, "And then what? Will the moon still break up?"

The Doctor responds in graphic detail, "Well, there'll be nothing to make it break up. There will be nothing trying to force its way out. The gravity of the little dead baby will pull all the pieces back together again. Of course, it won't be very pretty. You'd have an enormous corpse floating in the sky. You might have some very difficult conversations to have with your kids."

Clara interrupts them, "This is a life. I mean, this must be the biggest life in the universe."

Lundvik counters with facts, "It is killing people. It is destroying the earth!"

Clara continues, "You cannot blame a baby for kicking."

It is here that Lundvik's fear surfaces, "You want to know what I took back from being in space? Look at the edge of the Earth. The atmosphere, that is paper thin. That is the only thing that saves us all from death. Everything else, the stars, the blackness. That's all dead. Sadly, that is the only life any of us will ever know."

Unlike the Doctor and his Companions, Lundvik can see nothing but death in space. Regardless of what they say, she has already made her choice.

Our culture has become increasingly death-centered as we move further and further from our Christian origins and beliefs about life. Death is often viewed as "the end," or "all there is." Since we are all headed into this void, our lives here have no real purpose. Arthur Lindsley, senior fellow of the C. S. Lewis Institute, put it this way:

"According to the atheist, life comes spontaneously out of the cosmic slime. All life springs from inert or nonliving matter. Life comes from non-life through evolution. Our origin, in other words, is out of death. Since there is no life after death, our destiny is death. What then is the point or value of life?"[42]

Abortion is forgivable, even logical, if life has no value or point. Children are a *choice*. Not a blessing, a gift, or even a life, but a choice.

In "Kill the Moon," that choice is given only to the women. When Clara turns to the Doctor, with his hundreds of years of wisdom and experience, for guidance, he declares, "*We* don't do anything. I'm sorry Clara. I can't help you."

The Doctor, the self-proclaimed "Defender of the Earth," now denies any claim of the planet he has so staunchly defended, "The Earth is not my home. The moon's not my moon. Sorry."

He continues, "Whatever future humanity might have depends on the choice that is made right here and right now . . . Kill it. Or let it live. I can't make this decision for you."

Clara doesn't want to bear the future of the human race alone, and she feels unfit to make such a weighty decision. Even the inclusion of Lundvik and Courtney isn't enough. Like the pregnant girlfriend, friend, or wife, Clara wants some input on such a weighty moral decision from one of the most important men in her life.

The Doctor's dismissal of her is chilling, "Sorry. Well, actually, no, I'm not sorry. It's time to take the stabilizers off your bike. It's your moon, womankind. It's your choice." The Doctor plays the ultimate abdicating man, leaving the women to determine the future of the human race, saying it has nothing to do with him. It is *their choice*.

Unlike is role in "The Rebel Flesh" and "The Almost People," the Doctor doesn't champion this new life, even though he proclaimed it "beautiful" and "unique." Instead, as the seconds tick by and the moon collapses, he leaves at this crucial moment of Earth's history.

Proverbs 31 commands "Open your mouth for the mute, for the rights of all who are destitute. Open your mouth, judge righteously; defend the rights of the poor and needy."[43] As Christians, it is our duty to speak for the voiceless and defend the defenseless.

If we see "Kill the Moon" as analogous to abortion, it is Clara's role to speak for the voiceless. She continues to speak for the moon-baby even after she is abandoned by the Doctor. Clara doesn't want to choose between the moon and the earth. She also wants to understand exactly what would happen if the egg hatches.

Lundvik agrees, but her fear of the unknown, unwanted problem still trumps this. Even if the shell did not harm the earth, she's afraid of what the creature might do. Again, like Cleaves in "The Rebel Flesh," Lundvik uses specific language to distance herself "It's an exoparasite . . . Like a flea. Or a head louse." It isn't a baby, or even a creature. It's a parasite.

Clara flinches from this dismissive language, "I'm going to have to be a lot more certain than that if I'm going to kill a baby."

Lundvik fires back, "Oh, you want to talk about babies? . . . You imagine you've got children down there on Earth now, right? Grandchildren maybe. You want that thing to get out? Kill them all? You want today to be the day life on Earth stopped because you couldn't make an unfair decision? Listen, I don't want to do this. All my life I've dreamed about coming here. But this is how it has to end."

Lundvik sets the trigger. "I've given us an hour. There's a cut-out here. If anyone has any bright ideas, or if he comes back, that stops it. But once it's pressed, it stays pressed."

Still reluctant, Clara sends a one-way transmission to Earth:

"Hello, Earth. We have a terrible decision to make. It's an uncertain decision and we don't have a lot of time. We can kill this creature or we can let it live. We don't know what it's going to do; we don't know what's going to happen when it hatches. If it will hurt us, help us, or just leave us alone. We have to decide together. This is the last time we'll be able to speak to you, but you can send us a message. If you think we should kill the creature, turn your lights off. If you think we should take the chance, let it live, leave your lights on. We'll be able to see."

Time continues to count down on the trigger case, and the entire Earth goes dark.

Lundvik is firm, "We can't risk it all just to be nice." Nine seconds are left. "Sorry, girls. See you on the other side."

Clara smacks the cut-off switch, stopping the bombs from dropping, and "ABORTED" flashes large on the screen. She chooses to trust that the moon-egg won't destroy them, and save its life. Only then does the Doctor return for them. He whisks all three women into the TARDIS and takes them to see what their decision has done to the Earth.

He lands on a beach, and they all exit in time to witness the moon disintegrating as the baby alien spreads its wings. The creature lays a new egg (a new moon) before leaving, and the four of them watch in wonder. Lundvik turns to Clara, "Thank you for stopping me. Thank you for giving me the moon back." Lundvik is overcome with gratitude, and her wonder at space and creation has been restored.

They leave Lundvik to restore NASA, and Clara waits until Courtney is gone to confront the Doctor, "Tell me what you knew, Doctor, or else I'll smack you so hard you'll regenerate."

> DOCTOR: I knew that eggs are not bombs. I know they don't usually destroy their nests. Essentially, what I knew was that you would always make the best choice. I had faith that you would always make the right choice.
> CLARA: It was, it was cheap, it was pathetic. . . . It was patronizing.
> The Doctor: No, that was me allowing you to make a choice about your own future. That was me respecting you.
> CLARA: Oh, my God, really? Was it? Yeah, well, respected is *not* how I feel . . . I nearly didn't press that button. I nearly got it wrong. That was you, my friend, making me scared. Making me feel like a bloody idiot.

She continues, "Don't you ever tell me to take the stabilizers off my bike. And don't you dare lump me in with the rest of all the little humans that you think are so tiny and silly and predictable. You walk our Earth, Doctor, you breathe our air. You make us your friend, and that is your moon too. And you can damn well help us when we need it."

Clara doesn't feel respected, empowered, or important. Instead, she tells the Doctor to "clear off" for good. By giving her an impossible choice, and then taking away his support as her friend, the Doctor has betrayed Clara's trust. Regardless of the Doctor's motives, his decision doesn't make Clara feel independent or respected.

Likewise, when men leave the women in their lives to make important decisions alone, they betray them. When men refuse to take responsibility as fathers of aborted children, it is almost as bad as making the choice for the women. A bad choice is no choice at all.

The Biblical worldview of life asserts that we are created by the God of Life. We live earthly lives, die, and pass on to eternal life. To the Christian, life is a gift, and our eventual home is with Christ. It is this hope that answers the despair of a culture of death. It is only through Christ that our weakness can be made strong. "For we do not have a high priest who is unable to sympathize with our weaknesses, but one who in every respect has been tempted as we are, yet without sin. Let us then with confidence draw near to the throne of grace, that we may receive mercy and find grace to help in time of need."[44]

When discussing the sanctity of life, we must remember that earthly life is not our ultimate good or end. Our chief end, as put by the Westminster Shorter Catechism, is "to glorify God and to enjoy him forever."[45] It is only through Christ that we gain meaning and purpose in our lives. And only through Him can we understand the true value of the lives of others.

In conclusion, "The Rebel Flesh" and "The Almost People" contain some of the Doctor's finest moments as a defender of life. As art, they remind us of the worth and respect due to creatures created in the image of God. As C. S. Lewis writes in *The Weight of Glory*, "There are no *ordinary* people." Every person is an immortal soul headed toward glory or damnation, and worthy of respect.[46]

"Kill the Moon," on the other hand, vividly imitates an abortion scenario where every character is forced to act on their beliefs. By allowing the Doctor to abandon Clara in the name of "respecting her," or empowering her, he actually tears away his friendship and trust, leaving her vulnerable in a difficult time.

Both episodes reinforce the value and importance of individual lives. Though at times silly and melodramatic, "The Rebel Flesh" and "The Almost People" maintain that life is sacred, important, and unique. "Kill the Moon" affirms that life is the right choice, though not the easiest, showing the responsibility that both men and women have in the question of abortion.

God's image, reflected in His creation, is only a shadow of His glory. Though we are pale copies, the Bible maintains that we are more precious to God than any sparrows.[47] While the Doctor is fictional, his example is real. Life is precious. It is not a mistake, but a gift. Every person is created in the image of a God more immense, terrible, and wonderful, than television writers can fathom.

ENDNOTES

1   J. R. R. Tolkien, *The Fellowship of the Ring* (New York: Ballantine Books, 1981), 93.
2   He also apparently reminds himself of Gandalf, a "Space Gandalf." Unreleased scene between "Flesh and Stone" and "The Vampires of Venice", 2010. In "The Last of the Time Lords", Original Air Date June 30, 2007 the Master also refers to the Doctor as Gandalf.
3   The Doctor's many encounters with the Master, for example.
4   Genesis 9:6. All quotes in this essay are taken from the *English Standard Version*, unless otherwise noted.
5   Romans 13:4, Leviticus 24:17-23. In the Old Testament, there were "avengers of blood," (Numbers 35:19-27) but they were a part of Biblical society and government, and regulated by Biblical law.
6   Support for physician-assisted death is on the rise in the United States, with several state bills up for consideration. http://www.deathwithdignity.org/advocates/national.
7   You can read the Hippocratic Oath in full at http://guides.library.jhu.edu/content.php?pid=23699&sid=190964.
8   "The Day of the Doctor."
9   Ibid.
10 "A Christmas Carol."
11 Genesis 1:26-28.
12 Genesis 9:5-6.
13 Psalm 139:15.
14 "The Rebel Flesh."
15 Ibid.
16 For Sandel's arguments: Michael J. Sandel, "Embryos Do Not Deserve the Moral Status of Persons." Reproductive Technologies. Ed. Clay Farris Naff. (Detroit: Greenhaven Press, 2007).

Web: http://ic.galegroup.com/ic/ovic/ViewpointsDetailsPage/DocumentToolsPortletWindow?
displayGroupName=Viewpoints&action=2&catId=&documentId=GALE%7CEJ3010454212&
source=Bookmark&u=winn16583&jsid=9d3dbd680d5fa9920414a0d8b5b8baee.

17 "The Rebel Flesh."
18 Ibid.
19 Ibid.
20 Ibid.
21 Gilbert Meilaender, *Bioethics: A Primer for Christians, 3rd Edition* (Grand Rapids, MI: Wm. B. Eerdmans Publishing Co., 2013), 6.
22 *Frankenstein*, by Mary Shelley is a gothic novel about the relationship between an egotistical scientist and the monster he creates in his lab.
23 "The Rebel Flesh."
24 Andrew Pollack, "Cloning Said to Yield Human Embryos," *The New York Times*, January 18, 2008.
25 Meilaender, *Bioethics*, 124.
26 "The Rebel Flesh."
27 Merriam Webster *"Life."* 2014. 28 August 2014. http://www.merriam-webster.com/dictionary/life.
28 *The Declaration of Independence*, emphasis mine. http://www.archives.gov/exhibits/charters/declaration.html.
29 "The Rebel Flesh."
30 Ibid.
31 Robert P. George and Christopher Tollefsen, *Embryo: A Defense of Human Life* (New York: Doubleday, 2008).
32 Leon R. Cass, "Ageless Bodies, Happy Souls," http://www.thenewatlantis.com/publications/ageless-bodies-happy-souls. (Reprinted from *The New Atlantis*, Number 1, Spring 2003, 9-28).
33 Psalm 139:13-16 (Emphasis mine).
34 Exodus 20:13.
35 Genesis 9.
36 John Davis, "Sanctity of Life," http://www.ligonier.org/learn/articles/sanctity-life 1 July 2005. http://www.ligonier.org/.
37 Mary Wollstonecraft Shelley, *Frankenstein* (New York: Penguin Classics, 2003).
38 Meilaender, *Bioethics*, 9.
39 Episode quotations are from "Kill the Moon."
40 Mother Teresa, "National Prayer Breakfast Speech Against Abortion," February 3, 1994 http://www.priestsforlife.org/brochures/mtspeech.html.
41 1 John 4:18.
42 Art Lindsley, Ph. D, "C. S. Lewis on Life and Immortality," http://www.cslewisinstitute.org/webfm_send/705 (This article originally appeared in the Summer 2003 issue of *Knowing and Doing*).
43 Proverbs 31:8-9.
44 Hebrews 4:15-16.
45 *Westminster Shorter Catechism*, Question 1.
46 C.S Lewis, *The Weight of Glory*, 2013, originally published 1941 by the SPCK. http://tjx.sagepub.com/content/43/257/263.full.pdf+html.
47 Matthew 10:29-31.

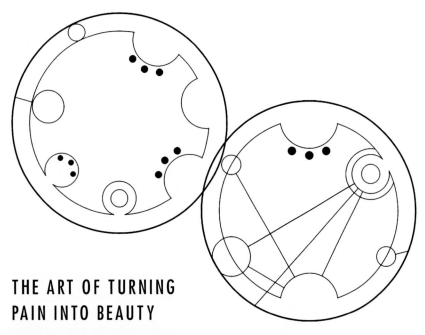

THE ART OF TURNING
PAIN INTO BEAUTY

SUFFERING: *Vincent and the Doctor*
ORIGINAL AIRDATE: JUNE 5, 2010

Not every brushstroke in the Velázquez masterpiece *Las Meninas* was made by the master's hand. The well-known painting depicts the Spanish Infanta, her retinue, and the painter himself through the eyes of its putative subject, the royal couple—whose reflection can be glimpsed in a mirror on the back wall. In a visual sleight of hand that may account for the work's enduring popularity, the viewer regards the scene, including Velázquez leaning out from behind his canvas, as if through the eyes of the king and queen. Said king was so impressed that he inducted Diego Velázquez posthumously into the Order of St. John, instructing an anonymous understudy to add the order's device in red paint to Velázquez's doublet in *Las Meninas,* a visible sign of royal approval that is often mistaken for part of the original painting.

This addition has always troubled me.

If there was one lesson the museum of my youth instilled, it was never to touch—let alone tamper with—the art. The Imperial Calcasieu Museum, a less impressive institution than its name might suggest, made up for its lack of genuine antiquities by treating what it did possess with extraordinary precaution. Even the not-to-scale doll of the early nineteenth century pirate Jean Lafitte, a local hero, was housed behind protective glass. Looking back, it's hard to imagine what further steps the Imperial Calcasieu could have taken if something as valuable as *Las Meninas* had fallen into its clutches, but I suspect it would have involved spools of barbed wire. Not that such measures were necessary. Uncultured as we were, the schoolchildren of southwest Louisiana would have known better than, for example, to dip a brush in red paint and daub an extra bit onto the canvas, even with the best of intentions.

"Of course," you might object, "none of you were kings of Spain." True enough. But let's face it: the king of Spain was no Velázquez. Paul Johnson tells the story—probably apocryphal, but I hope not—of Beethoven cutting a path through a crowd of oncoming German princes while the older Goethe steps aside to make room for them. "There are hundreds of princes in Germany," the composer quips, "but there is only one Beethoven!" Velázquez might have made a similar boast. If the king who honored him is remembered anymore, it is because Velázquez painted him.

Perhaps I've gotten the master wrong, though. This posthumous amendment might have pleased him, if he had know, in the same way a Pulitzer Prize sticker on the cover of one of my novels would not go amiss. The emblem of the Order of St. John represented the vindication every artist surely craves. Whatever doubts and difficulties plagued his path, whatever privations, no matter how often he struggled with the temptation to chuck it all in and get a real job, Velázquez at long last enjoyed the approval of the ages.

In this regard the artistic ego, so soaring and fragile, is no different than anyone else's. The need to believe our work matters is not an artistic motive, but a human one. We all want to know we haven't wasted our lives, that our sacrifices and suffering haven't been in vain. The language might have changed over time—where they longed for glory, we crave recognition, or worse, validation—but the need endures. Though I've never picked up a paintbrush, I can sympathize with what that symbol of the Order of St. John on Velázquez's doublet might have meant to the artist, because I can appreciate what it might have meant to the man.

You were right to pursue your dream. Your life made a difference. It meant something.

Even those of us who scoff at these longings where eternal rewards are concerned still feel them when it comes to our work, to the significance of what we've done in this life. During Velázquez's day, the life to come was still nothing to scoff at. The insignia of the Order might have meant even more to him, the king's favor bringing to mind the words of the good master from Christ's parable: "Well done, good and faithful servant. You have been faithful over a little; I will set you over much. Enter into the joy of your master."

I say *might* because, of course, we have no idea what Velázquez thought. It's not like we can travel back in a time to ask him.

Not every museum sequesters its treasures behind glass. When you're housing the bulk of what's left of the ancient world, as the British Museum does, you feel a bit less protective than the Imperial Calcasieu does of its Jean Lafitte doll. I learned this the hard way during my first visit to the British Museum, when I nearly missed the Rosetta Stone because some tourists were sitting on it to have their picture taken. No alarm sounded, no masked SAS men roped in waving submachine guns. I felt like a medieval monk on pilgrimage from the provinces, shocked at the lax complacence of Rome. The lesson I learned, the end of my cultural innocence: when you're overwhelmed by objects of reverence, there's no way to give everything its due.

I'm infused with a similar anxiety whenever *Doctor Who*, a show I've loved since it started to air on my local PBS station in the early 1980s, ventures into the historical past. Are we going to be revering this week's Rosetta Stone or sitting on it? The program's *laissez faire* attitude toward history mirrors that of the British Museum, in fact, sometimes honoring the past and sometimes trampling it—and at its very best doing a bit of both, as when the Doctor and Amy Pond visit the Musée d'Orsay and, peering closely at Van Gogh's painting *The Church at Auvers,* find a monster staring back.

What makes "Vincent and the Doctor" such a fascinating episode is its promise to resolve the question which, in the case of Velázquez, cannot be answered. When the Doctor and Amy travel back in time to investigate the mysterious creature in the painting, they find in Vincent Van Gogh the very archetype of a tortured genius, unappreciated by the world (including the waiter at the café terrace Van Gogh's painting is destined to make famous). If anyone can benefit from knowing history's verdict, it's Vincent, who's beginning to side with his detractors in thinking himself insane.

Only Vincent can see the invisible monster taking the lives of the people of Arles. The locals blame his madness for the deaths, but the Doctor and Amy believe him and eventually identify the beast. Together they corner it inside the Auvers church, where Vincent does away with the beast by stabbing it with the legs of his easel. In a nice touch, as the Doctor enters the church, he looks up to note a relief of St. George slaying the dragon, underscoring the metaphorical role of the church as a place for the cornering and killing of monsters.

While dragging historical figures into an action plot doesn't always end well, here it works perfectly thanks to the fact that Vincent's struggle—against the monster, against society, against himself—is a perfect metaphor. Helping Vincent conquer the outer demon helps him conquer the inner demon of uncertainty. Confirming the way he perceives the world literally also confirms Vincent's artistic perception. In a beautifully rendered moment, the Doctor, Amy, and Vincent gaze up at the heavens over Provence and, as the painter describes the scene, it transforms into *Starry Night*. "I've seen many things, my friend," the Doctor tells him, "but you're right: nothing quite as wonderful as the things you see."

Nobody sees what Vincent sees—but they will. Unable to leave without assuring him of this, the time traveling duo bring Van Gogh along to the Musée d'Orsay, where the Doctor asks a bow-tied curator (a stand-out cameo by Bill Nighy) for his assessment of Van Gogh's work:

> CURATOR: . . . to me Van Gogh is the finest painter of them all. Certainly the most popular great painter of all time. The most beloved, his command of colour most magnificent. He transformed the pain of his tormented life into ecstatic beauty. Pain is easy to portray, but to use your passion and pain to portray the ecstasy and joy and magnificence of our world, no one had ever done it before. Perhaps no one ever will again. To my mind, that strange, wild man who roamed the fields of Provence was not only the world's greatest artist, but also one of the greatest men who ever lived.

When that strange, wild man hears this verdict, he is in tears. Whatever confirmation he could have longed for, here it is. His suffering means something. It will give birth to the greatest beauty. The red emblem on Velázquez's breast is nothing compared to this. If future reward is what we work for, the knowledge that one day it will all be "worth it," Vincent can ask for nothing more.

"This changes everything," Vincent says on his return to Provence.

Amy agrees. Throughout the episode, the viewer's pity for her builds, because it's obvious Amy is in thrall to hope. Surely their intervention will change Vincent's life. The tragic history will be rewritten, and Vincent won't die the way the history books dictate, by his own hand.

"Just months from now, he will take his own life," the Doctor reminds her.

"Don't say that. Please."

There's no way Vincent can have experienced all that the Doctor and Amy have given him and still do a thing like that. Knowing what's in store, Vincent should return to his art with renewed vigor, pumping out new masterpieces at a prodigious rate, living and working long enough to enjoy the coming fame. Whatever was broken in Vincent is now fixed. Amy's belief in his salvation is absolute—there will be "hundreds of new paintings," she exclaims—but we know she is destined for heartbreak.

No matter how many times the Doctor lectures us on the unfixed nature of time—the possibility of altered outcomes being essential to the drama—even he concedes there are certain nailed-down temporal points, unchangeable fulcrums around which the rest of history revolves. Fans of time travel fiction know that assassinating Hitler to avert the Holocaust or leaving Van Gogh happy and well-adjusted, tempting as it may be, violates an unspoken prime directive of the genre. The implications are too weighty to be dealt with in the final minutes of an hour-long television episode.

When, after everything, Vincent still commits suicide, Amy is distraught. How could he still do it, knowing how much he is loved?

A profound question, only the story sets up the dilemma more effectively than the episode can answer it. When Amy tells him they "didn't make a difference at all," the Doctor's reply reminds us that his wisdom is, after all, the wisdom of television writers and not the words of a man who's traveled the universe and history through a dozen incarnations. "The way I see it," he says, "every life is a pile of good things and bad things. The good things don't always soften the bad things, but vice-versa, the bad things don't necessarily spoil the good things and make them unimportant."

No, indeed.

We work for a reward. A carrot is dangled and we reach forward to grasp it. Nothing worth having is easy to obtain, so we expect the hardships, and even welcome them. Not the suffering, perhaps, but even that can be endured for a greater good, hopefully in this life, though some of us reconcile ourselves to receiving it in the next. So how can a man like Vincent Van Gogh receive this revelation of his future reward and not be transformed by it? How can his life not be saved? We can tell ourselves that the genre forces this conclusion—in real life, he would be saved, but the story can't allow it—or we can tell ourselves that mental illness is to blame. Monsters vanquished, time travel, future exhibitions, nice as they are, don't constitute a treatment for clinical depression, and might even exacerbate the problem.

There's another possibility, though.

Perhaps the praise just isn't enough. Whatever we live for, whatever we work for, maybe it's more than just a reward. Vincent's brokenness goes beyond the need for validation, or for glory. He doesn't need a reward, he needs to be remade. This solution lies beyond the power of history or curators or time lords. It's hard to fix what you don't have the power to create in the first place.

At the beginning of the episode, the curator describes the remarkable final months of Van Gogh's creative output, and his life. What strikes him as particularly noteworthy is that these last masterpieces, which rank along Shakespeare's in the curator's estimation, are undertaken "with no hope of praise or reward." So what does Vincent work for if not these things? It seems to me he has a deeper desire to know and to be known. The specter of loneliness haunts him, so much so that the prospect of the Doctor and Amy leaving drives Vincent to throw himself on his bed and cry, "I will be left alone once more with an empty heart and no hope." Their companionship has meant everything to him, the feeling of being understood. It is this which seems to motivate his final period, though it cannot overcome his depression.

"We have fought monsters together and we have won," Vincent tells the Doctor. "On my own I fear I may not do as well."

I have sometimes wondered if, in the Christian sacrament of communion, there isn't an echo of what happens between an artist and his work. Here the creator and creature come together, the one inhabiting and sustaining the other, and in this communion we recognize a kind of knowledge. The apostle Paul even writes of a future point when he will know God, "even as I have been fully known." This idea of knowing and being known seems to lie at the heart of human creative expression. Or perhaps I've got it all backward and the artist and his work is just the metaphor—one of many—for the deeper communion envisioned in the sacrament. Either way, something more is at work than simply getting a reward. Vincent's last gesture turns out to be a gift: an inscription to Amy on a painting of her beloved sunflowers.

The biblical idea of what rewards are for turns out to be paradoxical. The saints are crowned not so that they will get something, but so that they will have something to give. The crowns aren't for wearing, they're for casting at the feet of the one who gave them. The reciprocal generosity at the heart of art turns out to be at the heart of all human vocation, too. You will be made whole so that out of your wholeness you may give back to the giver of wholeness. The message is not, *If you endure, you will get something.* Rather the message is, *If you endure, you will have something to give.*

What Vincent gave, the transformation of pain into beauty, could not have been given without the suffering he endured. It is no accident that the sacramental knowledge in communion is predicated not on Christ's power to erase suffering but his willingness to put an end to it by enduring it. In our broken way our sacrifices become a means to participate in this creative pain. Through this endurance we get nothing, but we do gain something to give.

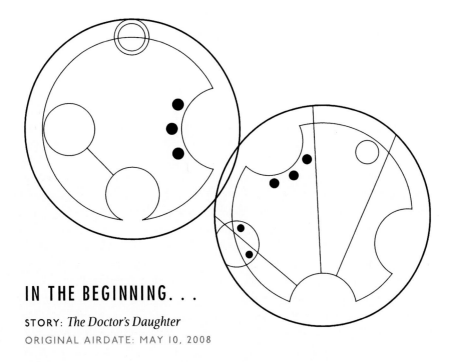

IN THE BEGINNING. . .

STORY: *The Doctor's Daughter*

ORIGINAL AIRDATE: MAY 10, 2008

In his groundbreaking *The Postmodern Condition*, philosopher Jean-Jaques Lyotard declares that one of the most important aspects of postmodern thought is a distrust of metanarratives. A metanarrative, Lyotard explains, is a story that gives people a model for understanding the world.[1] Examples of such stories include the Enlightenment and Marxism. In *A Primer on Postmodernism*, Stanley Grenz argues that this is one place where Christianity and postmodernism are in opposition.[2] By the simple fact of what it means to be a Christian, those who go by this name must trust one specific metanarrative: the story that is presented in the Bible when it is viewed as a whole. This story has been called the Christian metanarrative; it is the story that Millard Erickson, in *Truth or Consequences*, simply calls "God's Story."[3] This story is one everyone who grew up in church, any church, should know well: God created the world, humans sinned against God. Christ, God in the flesh, came, died and rose again in order to take away that sin. In *Mere Christianity*, C S Lewis calls this the formula that must be believed.[4] Intriguingly, one particular episode of *Doctor Who*, a story that includes its own metanarrative about a travelling Doctor who saves planets, presents a story that has quite a few striking similarities to the Christian metanarrative. *The Doctor's Daughter* tells a story about creation, fall and redemption that can lead the Christian viewer to reflect on the metanarrative that has shaped her own faith.

While Russell Davies, the creator of the rebooted series, is an outspoken atheist, it appears that this retelling of the Biblical narrative was undertaken quite deliberately. The book *Doctor Who the Writer's Tale: The Final Chapter* includes e-mails that were sent between Davies and another writer, Benjamin Cook, discussing various episodes of *Doctor Who* as they were being written. In the series of e-mails on *The Doctor's Daughter*, Davies discusses how his attitudes about religion shaped episodes that had already been aired at the time this e-mail was written, explaining that the Doctor is a non-believer who destroys the belief systems of others—sometimes with one sentence.[5] While neither Davies nor Cook specifically state that they intend to do this same thing with the episode "The Doctor's Daughter," the fact that this conversation occurs during a set of letters about "The Doctor's Daughter" makes this a pretty safe conclusion. Oddly enough, however, while the intentions of the creators of this episode may have been to debunk matters of faith, the overarching storyline actually repeats the story of creation, the fall, and redemption in a manner that is not only meaningful and touching, but also quite thought-provoking.

Here is how it happens: *The Doctor's Daughter* begins when the tenth Doctor and his companions, Donna and Martha, land on an unfamiliar planet. As soon as they arrive, a soldier grabs the Doctor and marches him to a machine that cuts out a bit of his flesh, extrapolates the DNA, and then generates a new person who steps out of the machine as a full grown adult. Donna names her "Jenny," short for "Generated Anomaly," because of her unique state of being. When the doors of the machine first open, Jenny sees the Doctor and recognizes him: her first words are "Hello, Dad." She never questions the fact that her father is something different from the other people who inhabit this planet. Throughout the episode, things are done to emphasize the connection between the Doctor and Jenny. For example, at different points in the episode both this daughter and the Doctor are described as "not impossible" but "highly improbable."[6] At another point, Donna grabs a stethoscope and proves that even though Jenny looks like a native of this planet, she has two hearts like her father. She is a Time Lord—she is of the same essence as the Doctor. At the same time, however, she has been born in exactly the way people on this strange planet come into being: not the way humans naturally come about, but through machines. She is, therefore, a creature with two natures: she has the essence of a Time Lord, and is therefore equal to her father, but she is also completely a creature of the planet she was born on, and is therefore one of them.

This should sound familiar to Christians. The Nicene Creed states that Christ is "of the essence of the Father," of the "same nature" as God the Father, and was "begotten, not made."[7] Christ himself declares that he and the Father are one.[8] At the same time, the Nicene Creed points out that Jesus was incarnate, and became human. *The Doctor's Daughter* begins by placing the ambiguous and enigmatic Doctor in the temporary role of God the Father, and his daughter in the role of Christ the Son. Like God the Father, the Doctor is older than this planet, wiser than any of the people who live on it, and works toward its good; Like God the Son, Jenny combines two natures into one.

As the episode progresses, the two different natures can be seen at work in Jenny. At one point, she explains to both the Doctor and Donna (and thus, the audience) the part of her that exists because she came into the world in the same way everyone else on that planet does: "Every child of the machine is born with this knowledge—it is our inheritance—it is all we know: how to fight, and how to die."[9] While this is her nature, the Doctor does the same thing with her that he does to all of his companions: he shows her a different way to live. Killing is always wrong. One does not have to fight, one always has a choice. One needs to stand up for those who cannot stand up for themselves. In essence, the Doctor enacts for Jenny the second of what the Bible calls the greatest commandments: love your neighbor, and Jenny not only learns from him, but models it herself. Just as in John 5:19 Christ declares that he does only what he sees his father doing, Jenny also does what she sees her Father doing. Jenny's similarity to Christ is not only in her essence and how she came into being, but also in the role she plays in the story of the planet she was created on.

When the Doctor and his companions land on this planet, they are immediately caught in a war zone. They are told that the war between an alien creature called "Hath" and humans has been waging for "countless generations." This is important: no one ever says anything about time, just about "generations." While this leads the Doctor, Donna, and Martha to make a certain set of assumptions, Donna uses a scientific method to discover that what is being called "countless generations" has really only been seven days. As the Doctor subsequently discovers by reading a book--the captain's log of a spaceship--a mere seven days ago two groups of people landed on the planet with the intention of populating it with a colony made up of both humans and Hath. The Doctor points out that because the machines can create new people quite quickly and the war kills them off equally quickly, one day could easily equal twenty generations. These generations have come into being and slaughtered each other so quickly that the original reason for the war has been lost.

The fact that only seven days has passed is important: the Doctor and his companions discover that the original colony was setting out to create a new world, and that world has now been created in both seven days and countless generations. This, of course, reshapes their understanding of what is really happening on the planet, and how they can go about stopping it. This also reflects the creation vs. evolution debate in a manner that suggests not a rejection of one side or the other, but a synthesis of both. It implies that somehow, in spite of what creationists such as Ken Ham or atheists such as Richard Dawkins insist, in some sort of postmodern paradox, they may both be right about the creation of the world. And just as this episode implies that these two extremes can be solved when more is known about how it all "really" happened and a synthesis can be found, the solution to the battle between the Hath and the humans can also be found in a revelation of the truth.

On the planet invaded by the Doctor and his companions, the space that has been created in the confusion between seven days and countless generations has been filled by a story that has been passed down—not exactly across time, but definitely through generations. A superficial interpretation of this story and the Doctor's handling of it may make it appear to be an argument against faith. One soldier explains to the Doctor and Donna why the Hath and the humans are fighting: "In the beginning the great one breathed life into the universe. Then she looked at what she'd done, and she sighed."[10] That sigh was supposedly captured and turned into a weapon: whoever has that weapon will destroy the enemy once and for all. After hearing this story the Doctor comments, "Right. So it is a creation myth."[11] He is told it is not a myth, but true. The captured breath is hidden somewhere in a lost temple. Later, after they have been thrown in prison for not believing what everyone else believes, the Doctor and Donna explain to Jenny that the whole story about the breath of life is a myth. The similarity between this story and the story of God breathing life into Adam cannot be missed. The Doctor explains that the story told on Jenny's planet is not true, but it could have some basis in something real that simply got distorted over time. He is bringing into question the metanarrative that has shaped the war between the Hath and the humans. The Doctor goes farther: he discovers the truth at the center of the myth on Jenny's planet: the "lost temple" is really a space ship, and the breath of life is really a "third generation terraforming device—an object designed for the colonization of otherwise uninhabitable planets." [12] He has now proven that the story that has given shape to the war, the metanarrative that gives meaning to the lives of all children of the machine, is false. It is an object that gives planets an atmosphere and causes plants to grow. The entire mythological system that gives force and power to the battle between the Hath and humans is proven by the Doctor to be based not in religion, but in a specific scientific act. When he has the attention of both the Hath and the humans, the Doctor explains: "Your whole history is just Chinese whispers—getting more distorted as it gets passed on."[13] This is exactly what many atheists believe the story of the Bible is: some ancient tales that were changed and passed on over time. The Doctor goes on to describe what a third generation terraforming device is: "It is from a laboratory—not some creator... it is used to make barren planets habitable. It isn't for killing, it brings life." [14] In this scene the Doctor destroys both the metanarrative and the religion of the Hath and humans on this planet. But he does not provide a challenge to all metanarratives—instead, the story of the terraforming device simply replaces the superstitious metanarrative of the natives with a superior metanarrative of science. And because one metanarrative is being upheld here, other metanarratives may also be at work in the text.

At least one other metanarrative peeks around the corners of the science-over-superstition storyline. The scene in which the Doctor and his companions reveal the truth behind the myth occurs in a garden. This is because the first thing that the terra-forming device created was a garden. Seven days of creation, life beginning in a garden: the allusion to the first three chapters of Genesis is present. And therefore, it means something. The way this episode parallels the story told in the first three chapters of the Bible goes much further. Just as God confronts Adam in Eden after he has tasted the forbidden fruit, the Doctor confronts both the Hath and the humans in their garden after they have both attempted genocide. In this confrontation, the Doctor sets both sides straight: it is irrelevant who started this war or why. Their world is only seven days old, and they have already messed it up. Standing in this futuristic, scientifically-engineered garden, the Doctor declares the war to be over. The Doctor demands that the two opposing armies lay down their arms and repent. The Hath and the humans have introduced sin into their world, and just as God walked into the garden declaring that evil has been done and passing judgment, the Doctor walks into this garden and does exactly the same.

At this point, the story once again takes a turn that should not be a surprise to those who know the Bible. Many Bible scholars have read in the Genesis account a foreshadowing of the sacrifice that does not occur until the time of Christ. This is seen both in the garments of skin that God made for Adam and Eve—something had to die to protect them—and in Genesis 3:15, in which Eve is promised that her offspring will be wounded in the heel while he crushes the snake's head. The sacrificial death of Christ that these point to is, of course, the central event in the Christian metanarrative. In "The Doctor's Daughter" there is also both a foreshadowing through a death as well as the sacrificial death of the offspring of the lawgiver. While the Doctor's companion Martha lands on this planet with him and Donna, she ends up separated from her companions and in the camp of the Hath. While the name "Martha" itself has Biblical implications, her sojourn among the Hath also results in a foreshadowing sacrifice. Martha is a medical doctor, and enacting what she has learned from the Doctor, she uses her skills to treat one of the Hath who has been wounded. Like the Good Samaritan, Martha has compassion on someone who sees her as one of the enemy. Martha models for them the life she has learned from the Doctor: the good and right thing is to take care of others even at risk to yourself. In doing this, Martha does what Christians are supposed to be doing: loving her neighbor. Seeing the value in everyone. One of the Hath soldiers appears to have learned something from Martha: because of her kindness, this Hath ultimately sacrifices himself to save her. This not only displays how living out the gospel can change others, but it foreshadows another sacrifice that is to come.

When the Doctor, standing in a garden so luscious that the viewer can almost smell it, demands that the two armies lay down their arms, almost everyone obeys him. One person, however, does not. The human general Cobb raises his gun, takes aim at the Doctor, and pulls the trigger. Jenny, first of the children of the machine to realize that one does not have to choose violence, Jenny, the child of the Doctor who is of his essence but who is also a child of the planet they are standing on and therefore very much the same as the person who aims a gun at the Doctor, steps in front of her father and takes the bullet. Like Christ, Jenny dies enacting what she has learned from her father. And just as Christ's death is the result of the sin in the Garden of Eden, Jenny's death is the result of a sinful act that occurs in a garden on her own planet.

After Jenny dies, the Doctor grabs the gun that someone had dropped and aims it toward the man who has just murdered his daughter. But instead of shooting him, the Doctor takes the barrel in his hand, says "I never would," and drops it. The lesson in forgiveness is now complete. He has spoken of peace and forgiveness, and now he enacts it. Instead of taking vengeance, he forgives his own enemies. With his daughter's body lying nearby, the Doctor lays down a new law for the planet. He declares himself the basis for this law, calling himself "A Man Who Never Would."[15] Just as he has forgiven his enemies, they must forgive each other. In other words, the Doctor himself does not destroy all metanarratives, but creates a new one.

Of course, this story does not end here. After the Doctor, Martha and Donna leave this planet, Jenny does what any self-respecting Christ figure should do: she comes back to life again. Laid out on a table watched over by one Hath and one human, Jenny suddenly sits up, says "hello boys," then runs to a spaceship and takes off into space. Like Christ, Jenny comes back to life and ascends into heaven. Those familiar with the television series will know that, since Jenny is of the same essence as her father, she has regenerated, but when mapping the two stories together, it works the same.

While quite a bit of entertainment may be had out of seeing all of the points in this episode that do or do not correspond to the Biblical metanarrative, ultimately, simply playing a spot-the-similarities game is not the point. It is possible that this episode does something more. In his essay "Sometimes Fairy

Stories Say Best What's to be Said," C. S. Lewis claimed that his Narnia stories existed partly to sneak theology and the story of Christ "past watchful dragons."[16] Those dragons are all of the things that keep people from really seeing and experiencing the Biblical narrative for themselves: cultural assumptions, learned prejudices, and anything else that causes a hindrance. It is possible that this episode of *Doctor Who* may do the same thing: as viewers watch this story about a creation, a fall, a sacrifice, and a redemption, they may find themselves thinking about aspects of the Biblical narrative in ways that they never have before. This may both serve to strengthen Christians and, for those who are not, open the door for new thoughts and conversations about the reality of Christ and what it means.

ENDNOTES

1   Jean-Francois Lyotard, *The Postmodern Condition: A Report on Knowledge*, (Manchester, UK: Manchester University Press, 1984), 47.
2   Stanley J. Grenz. *A Primer on Postmodernism* (Grand Rapids, MI: William B. Eerdmans, 1996), 163.
3   Millard J. Erickson, *Truth or Consequences* (Downer's Grove IL: Intervarsity Press, 2001), 283.
4   C. S. Lewis, *Mere Christianity*, (New York: Macmillian, 1944), 44.
5   Cook and Davies, *Doctor Who, The Writer's Tale: The Untold Story of the BBC Series*, 56.
6   *The Doctor's Daughter.*
7   *The Nicene Creed.*
8   John 10:30
9   *The Doctor's Daughter.*
10 *The Doctor's Daughter.*
11 *The Doctor's Daughter.*
12 *The Doctor's Daughter.*
13 *The Doctor's Daughter.*
14 *The Doctor's Daughter.*
15 *The Doctor's Daughter.*
16 Published in C. S. Lewis, *On Stories and Other Essays on Literature*, ed. Walter Hooper (San Francisco: Harper, Brace, Jovanovich, 1982), 47.

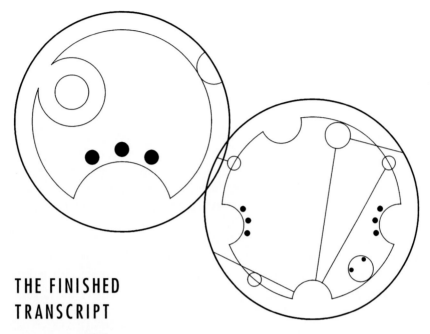

THE FINISHED
TRANSCRIPT

SCRIPTURE: *Blink*

ORIGINAL AIRDATE: JUNE 9, 2007

Sally Sparrow peels back the wallpaper in an abandoned house to reveal the words "BEWARE THE WEEPING ANGELS." With that cryptic command, Sally begins a marvelously strange, nonlinear journey that will take her places she never imagined.

Blink is a strange episode of *Doctor Who*. Though it's become one of the most popular episodes—introducing the Weeping Angels that have become some of the series' most famous villains—it was originally thrown together in a rather last-minute fashion (not to mention the fact that the titular Doctor plays a very small role in terms of on-screen time throughout the episode). But for some reason, the episode has resonated with people, and continues to function as an "introductory" episode. Author Neil Gaiman offered up this episode as an apologia for the entire series at San Diego ComicCon in 2011, saying,

> …look, there's a blue box. It's bigger on the inside than it is on the outside. It can go anywhere in time and space and sometimes even where it's meant to go. And when it turns up, there's a bloke in it called The Doctor and there will be stuff wrong and he will do his best to sort it out and

he will probably succeed cos he's awesome. Now sit down, shut up, and watch "Blink."[1]

Why is this episode so incredibly popular? Certainly it has something to do with the production of the episode. Carey Mulligan shines as Sally Sparrow, who far from being a throwaway supporting character, is the protagonist of the episode (and gets much more screen time than The Doctor, Martha, or any of the other characters). It's one of writer Steven Moffat's taughtest scripts in terms of dramatic tension and resolution, with just enough plot twists and turns to keep the audience eagerly on the edges of their seats and to reward repeat viewing.

It's also one of the more self-contained episodes of the series, as well as being one of the more high-quality in terms of production. But perhaps the reason it resonates so much with people is that it's incredibly good storytelling which unintentionally reflects a lot of truth about the way that God communicates with the world. Maybe something—whether it be Natural Law or God's image in us—dictates that people tend to like stories that reflect truth even when they don't recognize that truth.

After the introductory warning in the first moments of Blink, Sally continues peeling back the wallpaper and uncovers the words, "OH AND DUCK! REALLY, DUCK! SALLY SPARROW, DUCK NOW!" Though Sally doesn't understand this command, she obeys it—just in time to avoid a pot that flies through the window. Below the warnings on the wall, Sally reads, "Love From The Doctor (1969)." The rest of the episode follows the pattern of this opening scene—Sally receives somewhat cryptic warnings and instructions from The Doctor, and we, the audience (who are accustomed to being privy to the Doctor's opinions and detective work) are forced into Sally's limited perspective for the majority of this episode. We only know what The Doctor chooses to reveal to us, and we, with Sally, have a duty to figure out what it *means.*

In many ways, the Doctor's communication with Sally throughout *Blink* bears direct parallels to the way God communicates with us through Scripture. The connection is obvious—Sally is given a set of rules to follow so that she may prosper, and we are given scripture to follow so that we will prosper in our Christian lives. It's that simple, right?

On a surface level, yes, of course this is true in some sense—but the comparison goes much deeper than that. The Bible is not an arbitrary set of rules any more than The Doctor's instructions are merely meant to control Sally. And often, we don't see the immediate good that will come from obeying God's Word. There are parts of Scripture that are puzzling, complex, and even distasteful.

Madeleine L'Engle, author of *A Wrinkle in Time*, describes her struggle to understand certain difficult passages from the Bible (such as the dietary restrictions in Deuteronomy), and concludes that there are some things in life we cannot reconcile with scripture with our reason alone. "We can understand far more than we do," says L'Engle, "But complete knowledge and understanding is not for mortals in this life."[2] Listening to God's word means something more (though certainly nothing less) than merely *obeying* it. There is something deeper at work in our relationship to God's word.

The Bible is a story—a story that we are supposed to live out—and what The Doctor gives to Sally is, eventually a story. He explains what has been happening to her, that the apparently inanimate stone statues of weeping angels are in fact "creatures from another world," that they "live off potential energy" (the years you could have had), and that they can't act when they are being observed. This explanatory story sets the stage for what Sally needs to do in order to stay alive and become a part of the story, namely, "Don't blink. Don't even blink. Blink and you're dead."[3]

Once the Doctor explains the first part of this story to Sally, she knows that there is something bigger going on behind the cryptic warnings she has been receiving up to this point. She now takes initiative to figure out exactly what is going on. However, she can only do this because The Doctor has already reached out to her. We see God taking the initiative to reach out to people who are dead in sin and incapable of saving themselves (Ephesians 2:5). Scripture is the primary way in which God has chosen to communicate with us; it is incredible gift that God has given to us—his very word, which gives life and protects His people.[4] The existence of the Bible is proof of God's reaching out to us so that we can follow Him—so that we can love because he first loved us.[5]

The power of story is undeniable in human nature (which reflects divine nature), and that is why God, like The Doctor, has both given us a story and placed us in a story. L'Engle writes, ". . . my understanding is widened far more by stories than by provable fact. If it's provable, where's the mystery? Where's the faith? What is there to understand?"[6] As we mature in our relationship with God, our view of scripture changes—we are able to move beyond mere obedience (though we continue doing *at least* that) into a deeper relationship with God; we are able to open ourselves up to new ways of listening and becoming a part of God's story.

Further, the Word of God is more than a book; it is a person. John 1:1–3 says that "In the beginning was the Word, and the Word was with God, and the Word *was* God" (emphasis added). Through scripture, Christ is eternally present—a startling parallel to The Doctor, who is both alive in the past and the present. He is eternally relevant and unbound by the strictures of time and space, just as Scripture and the Word of God as embodied by Jesus Christ can never be relegated merely to the historical past, but are alive with everlasting relevance every day. As James K.A. Smith says in his book *Desiring the Kingdom,* "When the scriptures are read in the context of gathered worship, they are, in a sense, *enacted* at the same time." [7] Certainly, "time" for God is very different than the way we are accustomed to thinking of it; 2 Peter 3:8 says, ". . . with the Lord, one day is as a thousand years, and a thousand years is as a day."[8] This concept of Time seems similar to what The Doctor famously tells Sally in this episode: "People assume that time is a strict progression of cause to effect, but *actually,* from a nonlinear, non-subjective viewpoint, it's more like a big ball of wibbly-wobbly, timey-wimey stuff."[9]

Hebrews 4:12 further emphasizes the power that the word of God has in the present: *"For the word of God is quick and powerful, and sharper than any two-edged sword, piercing even to the dividing asunder of soul and spirit, and of the joints and marrow, and is a discerner of the thoughts and intents of the heart."* [10] We see a similar relationship between The Doctor and Sally in their videotape conversation. The video of The Doctor has been lying around since 1969, but it is only when Sally watches it in a particular moment of time that it makes sense; the seemingly random responses of the Doctor are a part of the conversation he knows she will have with him. When she watches the videotape with her disappearing friend's brother, Larry, this becomes clear:

> SALLY: He's the Doctor.
> DOCTOR: [on screen] Yep, that's me.
> SALLY: Okay, that was scary.
> LARRY: No, it sounds like he's replying, but he always says that.
> DOCTOR: [on screen] Yes, I do.
> LARRY: And that.
> DOCTOR: Yup, and this.[11]

This is the first time that the conversation, which has been played hundreds of times previously, makes sense, but The Doctor always knew it would. The Doctor is "eternally present" in that he knows how to communicate with Sally from the past, having already played a part in her future. It's an impossibly clever bit of writing that illustrates the nature of Scripture in a way that perhaps no other story has approached. The Doctor's words are uniquely *for* Sally's good in the same way that scripture is "profitable for doctrine, for reproof, for correction, for instruction in righteousness, that the man of God may be complete, thoroughly equipped for every good work."[12]

Understanding our lives as a part of God's story is crucial to the way that we live; C.S. Lewis, in his literary essay *On Stories,* discussed the relationship between free will and destiny—a relationship that is incredibly hard for human minds to grasp. The place where we are most clearly able to see the way this tension plays out is through story, as Lewis explains by citing prophecy-based stories such as the Oedipus cycle where the character's independent decisions bring about the prophesied ends. Says Lewis, "We have just set before our imagination something that has always baffled the intellect: we have *seen* how destiny and free will can be combined, even how free will is the *modus operandi* of destiny."[13] As Sally's apparently independent quest to discover what happened to her friend continues, we see the way that her investigation is inextricably combined with The Doctor's plan, and we, like Lewis, are left with ". . . a certain sort of bewilderment such as one often feels in looking at a complex pattern of lines that pass over and under one another."[14]

Sometimes, it's hard for us to see ourselves in the context of God's story, however. The Doctor's communication seems like random orders until Sally becomes more familiar with how to listen to and communicate with The Doctor, at which point he is able to tell her the full story of the Weeping Angels. In the taped conversation, where she has learned that she can trust in his communication, he tells her about the origins and powers of the Weeping Angels and what she must do *in light of* that story.

Similarly, the Bible is not a set of commands so much as it is the story of God's people and what to do in light of that story. In his book *Desiring the Kingdom*, Jams K.A. Smith describes our relationship with scripture this way: "Because we are story-telling animals, imbibing the story of Scripture is the primary way that our desire gets aimed at the kingdom." [15] Only once Sally has moved into greater maturity in her belief in The Doctor (i.e., once she accepts that he is a time traveler who is communicating with and helping her) she is able to comprehend this greater story. Previously, she was operating only on curt commands. It's crucial that we move beyond legalism into narrative. Christianity is not *primarily* a set of rules but rather a relationship and a narrative.

Unlike God, The Doctor is not all-powerful, and needs Sally's help in order to escape from 1969, the year where the angels have trapped him. Nonetheless, one of his primary concerns throughout the episode is empowering and protecting Sally to the best of his ability. This is why he gives her warnings and commands; from the very first scene where he protects her from the flying pot, he is looking out for her good. Just as not one sparrow will fall to the ground apart from God's will (Matthew 10:29), neither will Sally Sparrow fall if it is in The Doctor's power to keep her from doing so.

This is why God has given us scripture—for our good and His glory. He has told us His story and made us a part of His story. His word is eternal, and in it He is eternally present—we can trust in it, just as Sally learns to trust The Doctor.

"The grass withers and the flowers fall,
But the Word of our God endures forever."
–Isaiah 40:8

ENDNOTES

1   Neil Gaiman. "If this is Thursday then I must be at home." Neil Gaiman Blog. 7 April 2011 (accessed 31 October 2013). http://journal.neilgaiman.com/2011/04/if-this-is-thursday-then-i-must-be-at.html .
2   Madeleine L'Engle, *Penguins and Golden Calves* (Colorado Springs: WaterBrook, 1996), 246.
3   "Blink."
4   Matthew 4:4 and Proverbs 30:5, ESV.
5   1 John 4:19, ESV.
6   Madeleine L'Engle, *Penguins and Golden Calves* (Colorado Springs: WaterBrook, 1996), 244.
7   James K.A. Smith, *Desiring the Kingdom* (Grand Rapids: Baker Academic, 2009), 195.
8   ESV.
9   "Blink."
10 ESV.
11 "Blink."
12 2 Timothy 3:16-17, ESV.
13 C.S. Lewis, *On Stories* (San Diego: Harcourt, 1982), 15.
14 Ibid.
15 Smith, *Desiring the Kingdom*, 196.

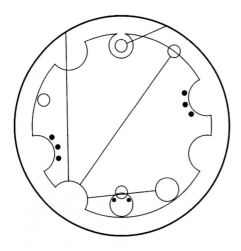

CONTRIBUTORS

J. Mark Bertrand is a novelist with an MFA in Creative Writing from the University of Houston, the author of three acclaimed crime novels featuring homicide detective Roland March: *Back on Murder, Pattern of Wounds,* and *Nothing to Hide.* The Weekly Standard has dubbed him "a major crime fiction talent" ranking alongside Michael Connelly, Ian Rankin, and Henning Mankell. He is also the author of *Rethinking Worldview: Learning to Think, Live, and Speak in This World,* a non-fiction guide to Christian faith now taught in various university and seminary classrooms. His first love, typography, led him to found Bible Design Blog (*BibleDesignBlog.com*), the most popular site on the web devoted to the design and binding of the Good Book. Mark grew up in the humid swampland of southwest Louisiana, but now lives with his wife Laurie on the steppes of South Dakota, where he is an elder at Grace Presbyterian Church. A longtime fan of *Doctor Who,* he is still dealing with the trauma of witnessing in his early teens Tom Baker's regeneration into Peter Davison. *JMarkBertrand.com*

Ned Bustard is a graphic designer, author, illustrator, and printmaker. His books include the *Legends & Leagues* geography series, early readers *Ella Sings Jazz* and *The Sailing Saint,* a historical fiction called *Squalls Before War: His Majesty's Schooner* Sultana, *It Was Good: Making Art to the Glory of God,* and he illustrated Steve Nichols' *The Church History ABCs.* Ned is on the board of ASCHA (The Association of Scholars of Christianity in the History of Art) and on staff with CIVA (Christians in the Visual arts). He grew up in Grace Reformed Episcopal Church and helped start Wheatland Presbyterian Church. Ned is the Creative Director for Square Halo Books, Inc. and Gallery Director of Square Halo Gallery. Ned and his wife, Leslie, live in the west end of Lancaster, PA. They have three daughters. He loves bow ties, and when he wears them to church, takes great delight in concealing a sonic screwdriver in the pocket of his houndstooth jacket. *NedBustard.com*

Sarah Etter is the second of five children in her family. Her biggest passion is literature, and her favorite authors are C.S. Lewis and Charlotte Bronte. She is in her third year of playing the piano, and her ninth year of playing the violin, and music makes her very happy. One day she hopes to become a history or literature teacher like her parents. She and her family attend Wheatland Presbyterian Church in downtown Lancaster, Pennsylvania. She has watched *Doctor Who* for a couple of years, and the tenth Doctor is her favorite.

Sean Gaffney is a playwright, screenwriter, director, teacher and producer. He now oversees the Regent University Script and Screenwriting MFA and Scriptwriting MA. He was the Story Administrator for Warner Bros. Features, editor of Drama Ministry Magazine, the Managing Director of Taproot Theatre (Seattle) and General Manager of Lamb's Theatre Company (New York). He has authored twenty-nine produced plays, four commissioned television pilots, two published books, as well as seventy plus produced videos, animation projects and short films (including for Big Idea, SuperBook, Yake Films and Globalstage). He received his BFA from Drake University, his MFA from Columbia University, and studied with Act One: Writing for Hollywood. Since the Doctor won't let Sean on the Tardis, he travels instead by clenching his hands in closets. *GaffneyInkwell.com*

Melody Green earned her Ph.D. in English Studies with a specialization in literature for children and adolescents from Illinois State University in 2008. She currently serves as the Dean of Urbana Theological Seminary in Champaign, Illinois, where she also teaches classes on Tolkien, C. S. Lewis, and other related topics. Dr. Green has published on a wide variety of topics, including "It Turns Out They Died for Nothing': Doctor Who and the Idea of Sacrificial Death" which can be found in *The Mythological Dimensions of Doctor Who* published by Kitsune Press. Another essay she is particularly proud of is "Scapegoating and Collective Violence in The Lion, the Witch and the Wardrobe, published in Palgrave MacMillan's *New Casebooks, C. S. Lewis:*

The Chronicles of Narnia. Melody has occasionally had the occasion to explain that while she does know the Doctor rather well, she never has gone by the name of River Song. Nor does she currently own a sonic screwdriver, since hers was confiscated as a possible weapon at the Bloomington IL courthouse when she went in to pay a ticket. On the other hand, when she is not reading, writing or deaning, Melody might well be hanging out at home with her life-size cardboard cutout of David Tennant as the Tenth Doctor.

Christopher Hansen is an independent filmmaker, and he runs the film and digital media program at Baylor University. His feature films include *The Proper Care & Feeding of an American Messiah, Endings,* and *Where We Started,* all of which are available on various video-on-demand platforms. He is the editor of *Ruminations, Peregrinations, and Regenerations: A Critical Approach to Doctor Who* and has contributed chapters to *Halos and Avatars: Playing Video Games with God* and *Too Bold for the Box Office: The Mockumentary from Big Screen to Small.* He is a deacon at Highland Baptist Church in Waco, Texas, where he lives with his wife, Sherry, their four daughters, and their mutt, Doc—who was not intentionally named for the Doctor but might as well have been, as Chris has been watching the show since he first saw Tom Baker as the fourth Doctor on Georgia Public Television. *HansenFilms.com*

Rebekah Hendrian is the manager, book buyer, and head bookseller for an independent bookstore in West Michigan. She writes for local publications and is currently working on her ninth novel. When Rebekah isn't writing, she is usually reading, knitting, travelling, or baking pies. She is an active member of Christ the King Presbyterian Church along with her parents and younger siblings. Rebekah has not knit the Fourth Doctor's epic scarf yet, but it is on her bucket list. You can follow her (and find links to more of her writing) at *rlhendrian.blogspot.com*

Tyler Howat lives in Bandung, Indonesia where by day he is a teacher and Curriculum Coordinator at Cahaya Bangsa Classical School, and by night he teaches Worldview in Film classes online at The Potter's School—all while attempting to write about pop culture and worldview. He constantly takes in whatever media he can—books, TV shows, movies, blogs—and uses them to teach his students more about the world around them. He once dressed as the Eleventh Doctor while in a friend's wedding party, and his deepest, darkest secret is that he sheds a tear each time he watches "Doomsday." You can read more of his ramblings at *Elementary, My Dear Reader: ravereader.wordpress.com*

Christian Leithart is a writer and filmmaker. He is a graduate of New Saint Andrews College, where he received his MA in Trinitarian Theology and Letters, which comes in handy when anyone asks him about the alphabet. His graduate thesis was entitled *Redeemed From Fire by Fire: Time in T.S. Eliot's Four Quartets*. He currently lives in Lancaster, PA, where he works for a video production company, writing everything from commercials to Bible curricula. His other interests include theater, language, movies, and the philosophy of Time. He travels the Twitterverse under the pseudonym *@cleithart*.

Fr. Joshua Lickter, the church planting Vicar for Incarnation Anglican Church in Roseville, California, attended Westminster Theological Seminary and Western Theological Seminary, before pursuing Holy Orders in the Anglican Church in North America. His eclectic congregation uses liturgy, art, and community (plus the occasional sonic screwdriver), to reach the disenfranchised in their midst. His favorite "Doctors of the Church" include Sts. Augustine, Athanasius, and Tom Baker. His work as a journalist has been published in *CCM Magazine, HM Magazine,* and *Reformation & Revival Journal,* as well as *East Coast Rocker* and several other arts and entertainment publications. He, his wife Rachel, and their son Elliott, enjoy traveling to Cons in costume, and being as nerdy as possible. *IncarnationMission.Org*

Leah Rabe is currently completing her bachelor's degree in Media, Culture and Arts at The King's College in New York City, where she also writes for the Office of Advancement. She also serves as artistic director for The King's Players—the school's theater group. She attends Central Presbyterian Church in New York City, and her home church is New Life Baptist Church in South Florida. Leah grew up in Cooper City, Florida, where she discovered *Doctor Who* during her awkward transitional teen years on her path of nerdy self-discovery that began with *Star Wars* and will probably continue forever. She cannot, for any amount of money, pick a favorite episode, but generally her favorites are any time The Doctor goes back in time and interacts whimsically with historical figures. *LeahRabe.com*

Carter Stepper is a teacher for Veritas Press Scholars Academy, where he teaches history and theology from the ancient, medieval, and modern periods. Besides being a teacher he is an aspiring writer, who wishes time would be more wibbly-wobbly in his favor once in awhile. He has spoken on Christianity and *Star Trek* and is currently developing a course on science fiction for high school students. He serves in his church is various lay capacities, including the occasional sermon, and hopes one day to be a minister in the

Anglican Church in North America. He, his wife Hollie, and their two children live in Spokane, WA, where he watches for wormholes and the arrival of celestial neighbors, while trying to sort out if androids do in fact dream of electric sheep. Carter administrates the *Bigger on the Inside: Christianity and Doctor Who* blog. *ChristianityandDoctorWho.blogspot.com*

David Talks is an Anglican minister in charge of the small parish of Lynchmere and Camelsdale in West Sussex, near Haslemere, UK. He came to faith while studying sciences at Cambridge University where he graduated with MA honours in Natural Sciences. After many years working in microelectronics and technology industries he trained at Trinity Theological College, Bristol with his wife, Rosalind, and graduated with BA honours in theology, and was ordained in 2006. He is also a certified Spiritual Director. They have two grown up children and a grandson in the Baptist, Pentecostal and House Church traditions, and David's mother is a Catholic—so he describes his spirituality as Evangelical-Charismatic-Sacramental-Contemplative. In his spare time he enjoys wildlife photography, messing about on their canal boat, watching *Star Trek,* and, of course, watching *Doctor Who.* He still owns a Tom Baker-style scarf that his wife lovingly knitted for him a few decades ago. It currently stands at 11 feet long, but is naturally dimensionally variable! *StPandP.co.uk/sermon-summaries.*

Gregory Alan Thornbury, Ph.D., serves as the sixth President of The King's College in New York City. He was appointed to the post in July 2013. The college focuses on the following areas as it seeks to prepare leaders for strategic institutions in society: Politics, Philosophy, and Economics (PPE), Business, Finance, and Media, Culture, and the Arts. *tkc.edu*

He previously held the post of Professor of Philosophy, Dean of the School of Theology, and Vice President for Spiritual Life at Union University in Tennessee. He is the author of *Recovering Classic Evangelicalism: Applying the Wisdom and Vision of Carl F. H. Henry* (Crossway, 2013). A Senior Fellow of *The Kairos Journal,* he is the co-author of two other volumes, and author of numerous book chapters, opinion pieces, and critical essays. He addresses a range of subjects, including philosophy, theology, music, spirituality, public thought, and the arts.

In addition to his work as a philosopher and theologian, he is also a guitarist, singer, songwriter, and collaborator. He can be heard playing guitar on the recent Thriftstore Masterpiece record (*SideOneDummy,* 2013) produced by Charles Normal on the track entitled "Railroad," featuring Isaac Brook from Modest Mouse. *Twitter: @greg_thornbury*

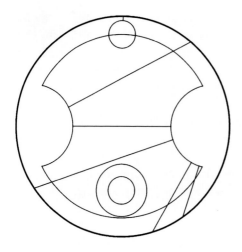

GALLIFREYAN WRITER

The Gallifreyan writing throughout this book is based on the work of Loren Sherman. She has written a program that enables you to type like a Time Lord. It can be downloaded for free at *shermansplanet.com/gallifreyan*. Learning to read this alien writing can be quite a challenge, but it is certainly much more enjoyable than learning the language of Tersurus (featured in "The Curse of Fatal Death," Steven Moffat's first televised *Doctor Who* script). For those whose Gallifreyan may be a bit rusty, it may be helpful to know that at the beginning of each essay the Gallifreyan on the left is the author's name and the Gallifreyan on the right is the topic of the essay. The Time Lord writing at the top of this page spells out "Jesus."

EXTRAORDINARY BOOKS
FOR ORDINARY SAINTS

INTRUDING UPON THE TIMELESS:
MEDITATIONS ON ART, FAITH AND MYSTERY

A compendium of the editorial statements from *Image: A Journal of the Arts & Religion*, these short, evocative essays constitute a new Christian aesthetic for our times. "... not since O'Connor's Mystery and Manners has there been such bracing insight on the pile-up where art and faith collide. This book will rev your engines and propel you down the same road." —*Annie Dillard*

IT WAS GOOD: MAKING MUSIC TO THE GLORY OF GOD

"Lively, engaging and eminently readable—this book shows that it is still possible to write about music in a way that enriches our experience of it. Above all, it will renew your gratitude to God for making such an art possible."—*Jeremy Begbie*

C.S. LEWIS AND THE ARTS:
CREATIVITY IN THE SHADOWLANDS

"Even fifty years after his death, C.S. Lewis remains one the most popular and influential Christian writers and thinkers of the twentieth century. So much has been written about him, one wonders what else can possibly be said. But this book is a fascinating exploration of Lewis's thinking about the arts, making it a must read book for anyone who loves Lewis and loves the arts."—*Mary McCleary*

THE END: A READERS' GUIDE TO REVELATION

"Alan Bauer spares us much of the speculative application that tends to show up in popular commentaries on John's Apocalypse. His goal is much more modest, that to equip us to read and study the book for ourselves. In this, he has succeeded handsomely. *The End* will be a helpful addition to the library of any serious Bible student." —*Report Magazine*

LEARN MORE ABOUT THESE
AND ALL THE OTHER TITLES FROM
SQUARE HALO BOOKS BY VISITING:

SquareHaloBooks.com